Chakra Divination™
Patent Pending
Cards & Charts Activity Book

Melissa Alvarez

Adrema Press

A NOTICE TO THE READER

The ideas and suggestions contained in this book are the opinion of the author based on her own experiences and are not intended as a substitute for psychological counseling or consultation with your physician. This book is not a medical guide. All medical references are intended to show the relationship between the body and the chakras, not as advice for medical problems or conditions. All matters regarding your health require medical supervision by a licensed doctor. The author and publisher assume no liability or responsibility for your actions or damages resulting from this book's information.

Text Copyright © 2010 by Melissa Alvarez
Chakra Divination™ Card Designs, Chakra Divination™ Chart Designs and Chakra Divination™ Card Meanings Copyright © 2010 by Melissa Alvarez All Rights Reserved.
All artwork is copyrighted by the artist and may not be reproduced by any means, electronic or otherwise.
Websites: www.ChakraDivination.com, www.MelissaAlvarez.com and www.APsychicHaven.com

ISBN: 1-59611-038-4
ISBN 13: 978-1-59611-038-0

All Rights Reserved. No part of the Chakra Divination™ method, including cards and charts, may be reproduced by any method whatsoever. Except for use in any review, the reproduction or utilization of this work in whole or in part in any form by any electronic, mechanical or other means, now known or hereafter invented, including xerography, photocopying and recording, or in any information or retrieval system, is forbidden without the prior written permission of both the publisher and copyright owner of this book.

Chakra Divination™ Card Art Designs and Chakra Divination™ Chart Art Designs by Melissa Alvarez
Chakra Divination™ Card Meanings created by Melissa Alvarez
Published by arrangement with the author.

Patent Pending

First Trade Paperback Printing: July 2010
10 9 8 7 6 5 4 3 2 1

> If you purchased this book without a cover, you should be aware that this book is stolen property. It was reposted as "unsold and destroyed" to the publisher, and neither the author nor the publisher has received any payment for this "stripped book."

ALSO BY MELISSA ALVAREZ

365 Ways To Increase Your Frequency
(Llewellyn Publications – Available Fall 2011)
You're Not Crazy, You're Clairvoyant
(Available Summer 2011)
The Essential Guide To Chakra Divination™
Chakra Divination™ Ultimate Balance Journal
Chakra Divination™ Cards
The Phoenix's Guide To Self Renewal
Your Color Power
Analyze Your Handwriting

BY MELISSA ALVAREZ *writing as* ARIANA DUPRÉ

Talgorian Prophecy
Beneath A Christmas Moon (Anthology)
Night Visions
Briar Mountain

All of the above are available at or can be ordered through your local bookstore or online at www.Llewellyn.com, www.CerridwenPress.com, www.Amazon.com, www.BN.com and other online retailers. Adrema Press books are also available at www.ChakraDivination.com, www.MelissaA.com and www.APsychicHaven.com.

Contents

Chapter One: Chakra Divination™ — 5

Chapter Two: Signs, Symptoms & Solutions — 6

Chapter Three: Crystals and Stones in Chakra Work — 10

Chapter Four: Chakra Divination™ Spreads — 11

Chapter Five: Chakra Divination™ Card Meanings — 15

The Suits
The Chakra cards — 15
The Problem Cards — 16
The Course of Action Cards — 20
The Solution Cards — 24

Chakra Divination™ Cards — 29

Chakra Divination™ Charts — 71

Chapter One
Chakra Divination™
Intuitive Chakra Readings

Chakra Divination™ is an ancient method of intuitive evaluation, which is used to energize, balance and cleanse the seven major chakras. Even though it's an ancient technique, it's also new, unique and non-traditional when compared to conventional methods of chakra work. This method was given to me from the higher realms as a way to examine the chakras through the use of intuition to uncover Problems, find a Course of Action, a Solution and obtain Ultimate Balance within each chakra, which benefits the person doing the reading on a spiritual level. The artwork and card meanings were also divinely guided. Chakra Divination™ is a system you can use when your normal functioning energy flow feels disturbed. Through the use of the Chakra Divination™ cards, spreads and charts you can learn how to focus on the chakras using your intuition and perform intuitive chakra reading for yourself and others. By following the information given in this book you can balance the chakras by doing Chakra Divination™ readings.

There are several products within the Chakra Divination™ line: *Chakra Divination™ Cards & Charts Activity Book*, which contains the entire text of *The Essential Guide to Chakra Divination™* (in a smaller font), plus the eighty-two Chakra cards and four charts you will use during the reading. It is designed to be an activity book, to have pages removed and lightly laminated before cutting out the cards. This isn't how most decks are presented to the public but by offering them to you in this manner you can create a deck that is personal to you. As you cut out the cards, you'll fill them with your own intention and program them to bond to your energy. This allows a deeper spiritual connection when you read for yourself or if you're reading for others. You can even write your name or other information on the backs of the cards before laminating them if you so desire. I purposefully designed the backs to be a light color, reflective of the purple and white of the Crown Chakra, so that you can clearly read anything that you write there. Yes, it's a different and unorthodox approach but one that makes the cards more personal and truly *your* deck, a combined creative activity between us.

The Essential Guide to Chakra Divination™ contains four chapters plus the meanings of the cards and explanations of the spreads. It is sold separately for those who don't want to create their own unique deck or for those who want to purchase a smaller book to carry with their deck. The *Chakra Divination™ Card Deck* is a manufactured card deck containing eighty-two cards. The charts are not included in the deck but will be available separately. *The Chakra Divination™ Ultimate Balance Journal* is a companion to the activity book, essential guide and card deck. With this journal you can record 100 readings and have a record of your chakra work. I decided to bring out a variety of products in this line and offer them in different combinations, separately and as gift sets, to appeal to different customer needs. You can always find the current product list on my websites.

Chakra Divination™ will help you make decisions about your life through chakra work. You will find the cause of imbalance and choose one of the ways detailed within these pages to tap into your inner self on a spiritual level, thereby bringing Ultimate Balance. Don't expect traditional methods or a conventional approach. This is a new way to diagnose what ails your chakras.

It is not the intent of this book to give a detailed history of chakras or to delve into the integral workings of the various philosophies studied and discussed around the world today. These philosophies are complex and require years of study. There are many books published about chakras if you'd like to do more research. However, you'll only find the Chakra Divination™ system within these pages. It is a unique method that has never been on the market before because it was given to me from the spiritual realm and I've never shared it until now. I don't claim to be a "chakra expert", I work with energy, and the chakras are energy so the two go hand-in-hand. Some of what I say here may have chakra experts disagreeing with me, and that's okay. This is what I know and what works for this method of divination. It's simple, but effective.

Before we get into the details of Chakra Divination™ I would like to give you a basic overview of the chakras and how they work because you'll need this information in order to use this system. The information I'm passing along in these pages came to me over the years as a slow absorption through discussions with others regarding what the chakras are and how they function. The actual method of Chakra Divination™ is the process that I was given from the higher realms to share with you.

Since we all have various belief systems, I am not going to try to be politically correct every time I speak of the higher realms. I'll just say up front that I believe in God, Angels, Guides and the power of the Universe. If your belief system is different then you'll just adapt what I'm saying to be in line with your religious views. Chakra Divination™ works for everyone, from all walks of life and any religion, because it's about energy.

Chakras originated within the Hindu belief system and the theories were later adopted in Tibetan Buddhism. The belief in chakras spread and now there are many different theories in numerous cultures. The theory of seven chakras is the predominant western view but it is only one among several. For the purposes of this book we will focus on the seven chakras most commonly viewed in the western world.

In order to understand and use the Chakra Divination™ method, you need to first understand each chakra and how it relates to you on a physical level.

What is a chakra? The term *chakra* is a Sanskrit word that means wheel. A chakra is a center of spiritual energy that moves in a circular motion, like a spinning circle or wheel, to form a vortex that draws in coded information within its vibrational level from any type of surrounding energy. You absorb information from your environment in the form of vibrations from colors, microwaves, and radio waves. You also absorb energy from other people and their auras, the energy they project and their moods. In turn, your chakras radiate your energy, which can be absorbed by others.

One of the main functions of the chakras is to transform energy in relation to your aura. Many psychics are able to see chakras as colorful rotating wheels of energy. The chakras are often represented as lotus flowers, each with more petals than the one below it as you move up the body from the base chakra toward the crown chakra. The lotus flower is symbolic of rising from darkness into the light. It's a symbol of rebirth just as the phoenix symbolizes a new life rising from the ashes of death.

You have hundreds of chakras within your body but there are seven central, larger ones that form a line along your spinal column to the top of your head. These major chakras affect us on a spiritual, emotional, physical and mental level. Each chakra is connected to a different organ or gland and those organs/glands connect to other body parts that have the same vibration through additional, smaller chakras located throughout your body. Each chakra has its own color association, its own intelligence center and its own vitality level. This means that each chakra moves at its own speed. Typically the Root/First Chakra rotates slowest and then the speed increases as you move up the spinal column toward the Crown/Seventh Chakra, which rotates at the fastest rate.

When learning to understand the chakras and how they work it is important to remember that energy is the key component. We are energy. Our chakras utilize the energy we collect, through different levels of vibration from the world around us. Chakras are stimulated by a variety of things including colors, gemstones and other energy. By using these items with intention you can keep your chakras balanced and in their optimal rotation. You must keep your chakras in their prime operating condition or you'll feel tired and moody or experience other problems like disease.

When the chakras are opened to the right level you will feel balanced, harmonized and at one with yourself and the world. If they are opened too much you will have an excess of Light Energy (also called Universal Energy) going through you (clairvoyants, psychics and mediums have to be particularly careful in this area) and this can be draining, exhausting and, after a while, if the chakra isn't balanced, it can completely wipe out your energy. If your chakras are too closed then you're not utilizing enough energy and this can lead to illness.

The goal with Chakra Divination™ is to help you become balanced on many levels. Sometimes it's great to sit and meditate for an hour or more while cleansing your chakras (and you can do that with this system) but in today's hectic world, we may need a quick alternative, a rapid chakra analysis and adjustment, which you can also do with this method.

Now let's take a look at each of the seven chakras.

The Seven Chakras
An Overview

The Crown Chakra: The location of the Crown Chakra is at the top of your head. It is associated with the colors violet, purple and white. It is also known as the Seventh Chakra. Its main focus is to unite you with the higher realms, your spiritual connections, your ability to *know*, and to keep you open and fully understanding your relationship to the Universe and God. The Crown Chakra is thought to be the link between the conscious and subconscious mind to divine consciousness. It is where you learn about your spirituality and to trust in Universal guidance. This chakra is also where you receive white light from God. It is your ability to know and the right to aspire to greater heights on many levels.

The Third Eye Chakra: is also known as the Sixth Chakra and associated with the color indigo. It is located in the forehead between the eyes. It is often described as a divine eye that has the ability to look up into the spiritual realms. The Third Eye Chakra is essential in developing your psychic abilities, in trusting your intuition and understanding your insights. This chakra is important in opening yourself up to self-realization and in releasing any hidden or negative thoughts that may be holding you back from reaching your fullest potential. It provides the means to see into other dimensions and to understand what you're seeing. It is associated with the pineal gland, imagination, dreaming and all things of a metaphysical nature.

The Throat Chakra: It is also known as the Fifth Chakra. It's associated with the color blue and is located in your throat region. This chakra is important in the truthful and free self-expression of your beliefs. It defines a person's ability to trust, not just others but yourself, both in life and on an inner level. Your creativity stems from the throat chakra. Are you organized and love to plan things? Then your throat chakra is in balance. Unorganized and scatterbrained? Then it's time to work on this chakra.

The Heart Chakra: It is also known as the Forth Chakra. What else would the heart chakra refer to but your ability to give and receive love? It is located in the center of your chest and associated with the color green (not red as you might expect) and your ability to love, forgive, and have compassion. It also affects your self control. This chakra is important in accepting yourself for who you are on every level. All relationships are influenced by our heart chakra.

The Solar Plexus Chakra: This chakra is associated with the color yellow and is also called the Third Chakra. It is located in the stomach area right above the navel. This chakra affects your feelings of personal power, your thinking abilities, self-confidence, ego and humor. It is the center of your emotions.

The Sacral Chakra: Located in the lower abdomen right below the navel, the Sacral Chakra is associated with the color orange and affects your ability to feel. It's also known as the Second Chakra or the Spleen Chakra. It is related to your ability to interact in social situations including intimacy. The Sacral Chakra is the center of your feelings. It is also important to your sexual and reproductive self.

The Root/Base Chakra: This chakra is also known as the First Chakra. It is located at the base of the spine near the tailbone. It is associated with the color red. The importance of the root chakra is that it is in direct relation to your ability to survive. It grounds you in the physical and material world. It is crucial in standing up for yourself, your personal feelings of security and the internal instinct to survive.

Chapter Two
Signs, Symptoms & Solutions
Are you out of balance? Fix yourself through focus.

I once went into a new age store and the owner looked at me and said, "Oh my! Your chakras are so out of whack!" I had no clue what she was talking about at the time so I just said, "They are?" For the next twenty minutes (the store was very slow that day) this lady stood in front of me with this golden gong that was about three feet wide. She held the gong close to me and banged on it, while saying "ommmmm" over and over again, moving around my body while she was working. When she was finished she told me that my chakras were now in balance. I thanked her, looked around a bit and then left. What she'd done had absolutely no affect on me and, quite honestly, I thought it was more than a little ridiculous.

The reason I'm telling you about this experience is this: while another person (and I'd only recommend a specialist not a store worker) who specializes in chakra work might be able to help you balance your chakras, it needs to be more involved than just banging a gong at you. In fact, you will see the most significant changes by intuitively looking within yourself. You'll access the chakra's information from your own spiritual core and this in turn will allow you to balance your chakras. To me, this is very personal and inner work that can give you great joy as you successfully diagnose problems and succeed in making corrections that will allow you to balance your chakras.

How do you know if a chakra is out of balance? Here are some of the warning signs that will let you know when something is amiss and that you should consider chakra attunements. After each chakra I'm including a quick reference chart for your convenience.

The Crown Chakra

One of the signs that the Crown Chakra is out of balance are headaches. Whether these are migraines, tension, or just a dull ache, any kind of headache will let you know that something is off kilter with the Crown Chakra. The more frequent and more intense the headaches are, especially if your eyes are sensitive to light, the more the Crown Chakra is out of balance. That said, you should always rule out a medical condition with your doctor if your headaches are debilitating.

Another sign that something could be wrong in this area is if you're having problems with your coordination. Do you find yourself suddenly being very clumsy, dropping things or tripping over your own feet? Have you noticed that you've got a rash? How about spider veins popping up? There's not much you can do about them once they appear unless you have a doctor remove them, but spider veins, varicose veins and other problems related to the circulatory system are all signs that the Crown Chakra needs work on your part to help bring it back into balance.

Are you feeling frustrated with your life, with those around you or feel that nothing is going right at all? Maybe you've even started having destructive feelings or gone into a depression. Do you feel that you life lacks joy and purpose? Are you irritable? Do you just want to bury yourself in a hole and let life pass you by? Are you obsessed with something or someone? Do you act indifferent to everything around you? These feelings are all signs that the Crown Chakra needs attunement.

There are other more serious diseases such as brain disorders and mental illness associated with the Crown Chakra being out of balance. Due to the nature of those diseases they will not be a topic here other than to say any brain disease or mental illness can be indicative of problems with the Crown Chakra.

Balance by: Focusing and writing down your impressions and thoughts will produce clear thinking and bring the Crown Chakra back into balance. Detaching yourself from the material world and opening yourself to the spiritual world also brings balance. Pay special attention to your dreams, visions and ideas. Write them down, analyze them. Use the color violet in every facet of your life. Realize that your thoughts and words are energy and that they have power. Then try to focus on the positive in every situation instead of the negative. Wear violet, purple or white clothing and silver and gold jewelry, eat purple cabbage, drink grape juice, use oils made from lavender flowers as perfumes. Practice using creative visualization and silent meditation to open the Crown Chakra. Allow white light to raise your inner self up to a higher level of spiritual awareness and enlightenment by connecting with the cosmic consciousness.

Chakra:	Crown, also known as the Seventh Chakra
Associated Colors:	Violet, Purple, White. Also Silver and Gold
Location	Top of the head
Signs of Imbalance:	Headaches, clumsiness, rashes, vein problems, frustration, lack of joy, brain and mental disorders, obsessions, lack of concentration.
Signs of Balance:	Trusting in yourself and those around you, being able to let go of control, having a positive attitude, feeling at one with God and the Universe.
How To Balance:	Focus and write; these produce clear thinking. Bring violet, white, silver and gold colors into your daily life. Thoughts have energy and power; focus on the positive instead of the negative.

The Third Eye Chakra

When the Third Eye Chakra, located above the physical eyes and in the center of the forehead, is out of balance you may experience rigid thinking. You will not be able to look beyond what is in front of you to see or accept your true psychic nature. Everyone has psychic abilities but if the Third Eye Chakra is out of balance you may experience a denial of these abilities, a doubt in your intuition, and avoidance in seeing things you don't want to believe in. You may put your experiences up to coincidence or ignore the divine completely. As a result, the joy you could feel on a spiritual level is disrupted. This is often a result of fear. Being afraid that others will look upon you differently, that you will be considered strange or odd by those closest to you can keep you from understanding your psychic self. We all may have experienced these doubts and fears at some point in our lives. I know I have.

There is also the fear of being consumed by all things psychic and spiritual when the Third Eye Chakra is too open. You may have met someone like this in your life. Someone who eats, breathes and lives everything of a metaphysical or new age nature and tries to shove it down your throat. They never talk about anything else and easily brush off your accomplishments to tell you about their own. Balance is important in this situation and can only be found when fear and feelings of being *all powerful* are kept in balance. Modesty and honesty are necessary for balance and to make and keep friends.

An imbalance in the Third Eye Chakra can also make you fear other things in your life like relationships, business success and obtaining the things you deserve. It can make you feel unworthy of happiness or make you egotistical and a know-it-all. This is your fear manifesting in an unconstructive manner. Living in a fantasy world, having problems thinking clearly and a lack of concentration are common problems when this chakra is out of balance. You may also be selfish and have negative energy around you, which can manifest as headaches, eyestrain and other vision problems. This chakra affects the eyes, face, brain, lymphatic and endocrine systems.

When the Third Eye chakra is balanced you will no longer feel a necessity for material things in life, the fear of death will disappear, you will accept your psychic abilities and may even astral travel, experience telepathy and consciously connect with your past lives and people in your current life who have shared past lives with you. You will communicate easily with your guides and may even develop mediumistic abilities. The Third Eye Chakra and the Crown Chakra are very closely linked. When both are open and in balance you will find that others notice your psychic abilities and spirituality. When this happens people you don't know will be attracted to you. They'll want to share their deepest, darkest secrets with you, a complete stranger, because they can sense your connection with divine consciousness.

Balance by: Acceptance, being consciously aware. There are many times when you will experience things of a psychic or paranormal nature. It is very easy to dismiss such events as your imagination or as less than what it truly is because of fears and disbelief. When you concentrate on recognizing the specific fear that is holding you back from being the most balanced and spiritual person that you can be, then you will begin to accept and fully experience the true nature of your soul. You can release that fear and bring balance to the chakra. The color indigo will help you balance the Third Eye Chakra if you incorporate it into your surroundings, your clothing, jewelry, food and drink.

Chakra:	Third Eye, also known as the Sixth Chakra
Associated Color:	Indigo
Location:	Middle of forehead above and between the eyes.
Signs of Imbalance:	Vision problems, blindness, eyestrain, headaches.
Signs of Balance:	Lack of need for material things, fears disappear, connection with your own psychic abilities.
How To Balance:	Accept your inner self and true nature. Conscious awareness.

The Throat Chakra

This is your center of communication. When the Throat Chakra is out of balance your words will not be spoken honestly or with confidence. You may leave out information or talk and tell too much without thinking about what you are doing. Basically it's a case of shoving your foot as far down your throat as you can get it or babbling like an idiot without making any sense. You speak before you think and may regret your words later.

Did you know that anger is stored in the throat? When this chakra is out of balance you will hold onto your anger and it will silently sit there in the throat chakra, spinning away, growing stronger until eventually it causes physical problems such as hoarseness, laryngitis or habits such as grunting or clearing your throat. The throat is also the place where anger is released. By acknowledging the reasons behind your anger, even an unconscious seething anger that grows slowly, you will be able to recognize the emotion and release it.

This chakra being out of balance can also cause you to be timid, quiet and feel weak or stupid when you hear yourself talk. You may stumble over your sentences, repeat what you're saying and be easily frustrated with the way you're presenting yourself, knowing it's not really the way you are. On the other hand, you may be a motor mouth who talks too much and who is overly opinionated. You may develop ear infections or sore throats, skin rashes or acne, hyperthyroidism or hypothyroidism and you could have upper back and shoulder problems. When this chakra is in balance you speak with fluency and will feel inspired and creative.

Balance by: Acknowledging that you are a clear communicator. Focus on clearing any clutter from your throat region. Concentrate on any anger that you may be unconsciously holding inside of you from past experiences. Face the anger, acknowledge it and then release it. There's nothing anger can do except hold you back or make you unappealing to others. If the anger is against someone who has hurt you just remember that what goes around comes back around and they chose their own life experience just as you did. When you hold onto anger against them you are only preventing yourself from learning your lessons in this lifetime. Release this anger and you'll find that you will become a much better communicator and a more balanced person; otherwise, you're only hurting yourself.

Blue is the color that helps to balance the Throat Chakra. One of my favorite ways to balance this chakra with color is by visiting the ocean and staring into its blue depths as I focus on releasing clutter from my throat region. While it's not always practical to take a trip to the sea, you can also use a picture of the ocean or an island screensaver on your computer. It's all about how well you focus and your intention behind the association of color when achieving balance.

Chakra:	Throat Chakra, also known as the Fifth Chakra
Associated Color:	Blue
Location:	Throat
Signs of Imbalance:	Ear infections, sore throats, colds, acne, thyroid problems.
Signs of Balance:	Clear speaking, inspiration and creativity.
How To Balance:	Acknowledge your ability to communicate clearly.

The Heart Chakra

What happens when your heart breaks? You are overwhelmed with painfully sad feelings. This is the same thing that happens when the Heart Chakra is out of balance. You experience feelings of sadness, loneliness and worthlessness. It becomes increasingly difficult to open yourself up to experience the love and friendship that others want to offer. You may not feel worthy of receiving love or may be afraid to love again after being hurt due to the fear that you will be hurt again. You have problems letting go, which can result in trying to control everything in your surroundings. You become critical, withdraw and feel sorry for yourself.

On the other hand, if you allow your heart chakra to open too much you may feel as if you have to handle everything yourself, carrying the weight of the world on your shoulders. You'll try to be everything for everyone, leaving no time for yourself. This will eventually backfire and boy will you know it when it does because you'll feel resentment, as if you're all alone with no help. You may feel unappreciated and isolated. When you're dealing with the Heart Chakra the most important element is keeping the fine balance between closing it off completely and opening it too much. This is the hardest chakra to keep in balance because it is emotional and based on the abundance or lack of love. Keeping everything in moderation is a good philosophy to follow when working with this chakra.

Love is indeed the key element when we're talking about the Heart Chakra. It is the area of your divine spiritual growth. It gives you the ability to give and receive love. It houses your love, ideals, spirituality, resilience, compassion and determination. It is the center for loving yourself and, in turn, loving others.

The Heart Chakra is the connection between your body, mind and spirit. When this chakra is out of balance you may feel it in your chest or between your shoulder blades. You may experience physical problems including heart palpitations, high blood pressure, heart attack, angina, panic attacks, difficulty breathing, insomnia, poor circulation, tension in your upper back and an overall tiredness. When this chakra is balanced physical ailments disappear and you feel loving, happy, friendly, compassionate, nurturing, empathic, and will look for the positive, good things around you instead of the negative. There will be a lack of physical pain in the heart region.

Balance by: Forgiving those that have hurt you in the past, allowing yourself to feel the love you truly deserve and releasing any negative emotions that you've clung to out of fear; these are the first things you should do to bring this chakra into balance. Focus on nurturing yourself so that you can feel nurturing toward others. Most of all - *relax*. Stress can cause the Heart Chakra to close, especially when you imagine slights and feelings from others that may not exist or may not be directed at you. Don't take everything that happens in your life as a personal attack against you. Allow yourself to rely on your own resilience and spirituality so that you can rebound from heartbreak. Wear green clothing, eat lots of green fruits and vegetables, and drink green tea. Wear a long jade pendant that hangs low on your chest and over your heart. Before wearing it don't forget to cleanse and program the pendant to balance your heart chakra (details on cleansing, dedicating and programming stones and crystals are addressed later in this book).

Chakra:	Heart, also known as the Fourth Chakra
Associated Color:	Green
Location	Heart region.
Signs of Imbalance:	Physical problems in the heart, chest and upper back, poor circulation, overall tiredness.
Signs of Balance:	You will feel happy, loving, friendly, more compassionate, nurturing, and empathic. You'll look for the positive and good in situations you're involved in and in those around you.
How To Balance:	Forgive past hurts, feel love and release negative emotions.

The Solar Plexus Chakra

The Solar Plexus Chakra is one of your power centers. This chakra allows you to reach your fullest potential. It is your strong will, your valiant and heroic nature. When your power center is out of balance you can turn into a bundle of nerves. You may feel queasy, have butterflies, or be plain out and out nauseous. You may feel powerless to control the events in your life and because you feel that way, in turn, you'll act that way. Instead of finding your own personal power, you may try to tap into the positive energy of others. Look within yourself. When this chakra is in balance you are motivated, energetic and strive to be all that you can be in every aspect of your life. On the other side of the scale, if this chakra is too open you may be overly confident and come across as a stuck-up jerk to those around you, or feel as if you have to be dominant and in control of all people and situations in your life. You thrive on "keeping up with the Joneses" and you may be overly critical and spiteful to others.

This chakra is also the place of ego and can work in extreme opposites. It can cause a loss of self esteem or an overblown ego. It also regulates your passions, impulses and is an important key in your overall strength. When it's out of balance you may get confused easily and get mixed signals from others. You might think they're trying to control you or manipulate you when they're not or you may worry about other people's opinion of your life. When this chakra is in balance you will not give these things so much importance and will find that you enjoy taking on new challenges regardless of what other people think of you, your decisions and actions.

The Solar Plexus Chakra is also the center for traveling to the astral plane, for spirit guide contact and of psychic development. It connects to the Third Eye Chakra and when both are in balance; you will find that your Crown Chakra will open even more to bring you enlightenment.

The body parts that are affected by the Solar Plexus Chakra are the digestive system, liver, gall bladder, small intestine, pancreas and the stomach. The resulting problems of this chakra being out of balance are stomach and digestive ailments, diabetes, food allergies, liver and pancreatic problems and nervousness.

Balance by: Focusing on your inner self and on regaining your unique, inner personal power. When you're able to examine your emotions and how you feel about your life, you'll be able to balance your Solar Plexus Chakra. Look at past situations that you have experienced to determine what is taking your personal power from you and then come to terms with those situations and release any negative energies associated with them. For example, if a bad relationship has drained your personal energy levels, leaving your power center at an all time low, then you'll need to look at that relationship with acceptance and understanding on both your part and from the point of view of the other person involved. Once you examine the relationship as an outsider looking in, you'll be able to sort through it and resolve any leftover feelings in your heart and mind. This in turn will allow you to release the situation and bring your Solar Plexus Chakra back into balance. The color yellow is associated with this chakra so by adding more yellow into your daily activities you will be able to balance to this chakra faster.

Chakra:	Solar Plexus, also known as the Third Chakra
Associated Color:	Yellow
Location:	Center of the stomach area below the ribcage and above the navel.
Signs of Imbalance:	Stomach and digestive ailments, queasiness, nausea, diabetes, food allergies, liver and pancreas problems, nervousness. Being egotistical and a know-it-all.
Signs of Balance:	Motivated, energetic and strives to reach fullest potential.
How To Balance:	Regain your unique inner personal power. Examine your emotions and how you feel about your life.

The Sacral Chakra

The Sacral Chakra is responsible for your feelings of self-worth. It governs your confidence in your own creativeness and how you relate to others. If it's out of balance you may suppress your emotions and close yourself off from others. This can lead to manipulative feelings that may eventually come out in an explosive and violent manner. You may feel guilty, have a hard time finding pleasure in life and refuse to accept even the smallest changes, overreacting when change is forced upon you. If it's too open you may feel like you have to be the center of attention. Then you do everything possible to draw attention to yourself through actions that may not necessarily be your true nature.

When the Sacral Chakra is out of balance so is your creativity and sexual energy, it will feel like feast or famine. You'll find that you either have a lack of sexual desire or you're a horndog who can't get enough. You're either overflowing with creativity or you can't grasp a new idea if it were hitting you over the head and staring you in the face at the same time.

If your Sacral Chakra is blocked you may also have physical problems to go along with it. These could be kidney problems, bowel problems (constipation or diarrhea), muscle spasms, night cramps in the legs or feet, problems with the sexual organs and intestinal irritations or disease. Early detection and understanding is important in correcting the problem and balancing the chakra as soon as possible.

When this chakra is in balance you will become more confident but not overbearing, you'll feel less guilt, more enjoyment of your life overall and you'll be able to control your emotions.

Balance by: Evaluating your self worth and your actions. Are your sexual behaviors out of line and to the extreme, as in feast or famine? Do you doubt yourself? Are you prone to drama? These are some of the types of questions that you should ask yourself. At the base of all these actions are your feelings about what you deserve out of life and how worthy or unworthy you feel about yourself. Bring orange into your life, eat some citrus, and wear orange clothing. It will aid you during the evaluation and balancing of this chakra.

Chakra:	Sacral, also known as the Second Chakra
Associated Color:	Orange
Location:	Two inches below the navel.
Signs of Imbalance:	Blocked thinking and creativity. Lack of sexual drive or being too sexually active. Going to extremes in situations and being reckless in your actions. Obsessive sexual thoughts, lack of energy, emotionally explosive, manipulative behavior. Kidney, bladder, lower back and intestinal problems.
Signs of Balance:	Expressiveness, abundance of new ideas, free flow of emotions, a balance in sexual activity.
How To Balance:	Evaluate your self-worth.

The Root/Base Chakra

Housed at the base of your spine (tailbone) this chakra is what grounds you to the Earth and binds you to the physical world. The Root/Base Chakra, also called the First Chakra, is what gives you the energy and the confidence you need when you are trying to be successful in the physical world and increasing your material possessions. This chakra is also associated with sexual energy and can have the same actions, emotions and problems as those associated with the Sacral Chakra.

When this chakra is out of balance you will feel as if you don't belong in your body, you don't feel connected with your material things and it's easy for others that don't have good intentions to take advantage of your generosity. Some may even try to rob you blind and you won't know what hit you until it's too late. You may be dependent on others, clingy and possessive because you feel that you can't exist without them. You've lost your sense of self and grab onto the physical because it helps you feel grounded again. You have abandonment issues and that fear leads to anxiety, frustration and feelings of insecurity. You'll find yourself reaching out to anything and anyone that could possibly ground you again, even if you don't realize that's what you're doing, yet you don't really trust those around you. Imagine a person falling from an airplane into a forest without a parachute and grasping at every limb and branch within their reach on the way down. That's what happens when the Root Chakra is out of balance on an emotional level. The physical problems associated with a Root/Base Chakra imbalance are weight problems (too skinny or too fat), sexual problems (impotency or being overly sexual), lower back and leg disorders, muscle cramps in the legs and hip problems.

When this chakra is in balance you will feel secure and safe in your own skin and in your relationships with others. You are deeply rooted in the present and don't find yourself constantly looking to the past or dreaming about the future. Instead, you set goals that will help you obtain the things you want and you will work hard to achieve those goals. You will live more in the moment.

Balance by: Trust in yourself. Use creative visualization during meditation to ground yourself back to the Earth. Draw strength from the Earth and know that only you have the power to release fear and bring security back into your life. You are a spiritual being and when you're able to ground yourself to this plane of existence and open yourself up to your spiritual side, you'll find that you can achieve anything your heart desires and be a balanced person in all areas of your life.

Chakra:	Root, also known as the First Chakra
Associated Color:	Red, brown and black.
Location:	Base of your spine, tailbone.
Signs of Imbalance:	Anxiousness, insecurity, frustration, obesity, anorexia nervosa, problems with the sexual organs, hips, legs and lower back.
Signs of Balance:	Feeling safe and secure, an increased drive and determination to succeed, sexual energy, feeling connected with your body.
How To Balance:	Trust in yourself.

Chapter Three
Crystals and Stones in Chakra Work
A popular method

I'm not going to get into the complexities of working with crystals and stones because that's not the subject of this book. However, I am briefly mentioning this method because it is one of the most popular ways of healing, attuning and balancing the chakras. You can use crystals, stones and a pendulum (if you prefer) with your Chakra Divination™ charts so it's important for you to know how to prepare them for work with the charts.

Since there are specific colors associated with each chakra it is only natural that a corresponding crystal or stone of a similar color would be associated with chakra balancing. When you select your stones or crystals to be used during this process you will want to cleanse, dedicate and then program them prior to use.

Intention is of utmost importance when you're cleansing, dedicating and programming your crystals. Focus on the crystal and intend that the energy from the water, sun or moon will transform any negative energy held within the crystal/stone into positive energy. This re-energizes the crystal.

To cleanse a crystal or stone you can hold it under running water from your sink and then allow it to air dry in the sun. My favorite way to cleanse my crystals and stones is to put them in a bag that water can get through but the crystals/stones can't get out of (a small mesh bag works best), then I go to the beach, tie the bag to my lower leg and then walk in the ocean. I always walk in water that's deep enough for the bag to be totally immersed so it floats along behind my leg without banging on the sea bed. This is easiest to do on days when the ocean is calm. If there are waves coming in you have to walk past their breaking point or chance getting knocked off balance. Afterwards, I rinse the crystals and stones in regular water from the beachside shower and then allow them to dry naturally by spreading them out across the table on my back deck. If you don't live near the ocean this isn't a practical step for you but you can make sea water yourself by using tap water and sea salt purchased from a health food or grocery store. Mix these two items together, immerse your crystals/stones, and then let them bathe for an hour or two before rinsing with tap water and letting them air dry.

One word of caution when cleansing, some crystals and stones will dissolve in water. Research the ones you've chosen to see if they should be submerged in water or not before you cleanse them. If not, you should use an alternate method to cleanse them or you'll end up with a bunch of particles in the bottom of the water dish.

Now that your crystal/stone has been cleansed, the next step is dedication. This is when you hold it in the palms of your hands and surround it with white light. Now state that the crystal/stone is to only be used for the highest good, with guidance from the Universe for fulfilling its greatest purpose, and with pure unconditional love and God's white light. Ask your guides and angels to protect the crystal in its work for you. By doing this you are giving purpose to the crystal for doing only positive and good. Once you dedicate the crystal it should be left all day in the sun or all night under the light of the moon to energize and purify it.

Programming, the final step, is when you state the intended use for the crystal and you attune yourself to its energy. This should be stated very precisely and not generalized. First you connect with the crystal/stone on an intuitive level and let yourself attune to its energy as it attunes to you. While you're doing this you should also listen to your guides and any advice they offer before actually stating the crystal/stone's purpose.

Once you have what you want to say fixed in your mind and you feel connected with the crystal/stone, then state your intention out loud in a firm clear voice. Say it repeatedly until you feel that the crystal/stone has accepted your intended use for it and that the programming is complete. Now, put the crystal away in the place where you will normally keep it. When you separate from the crystal by putting it away, your energy detaches from it. Then on a daily or weekly basis take it out and ask it to transfer its energy to you as you pick it up. You can place it at a specific place on your body to work directly with the corresponding chakra or you can simply hold it in your hand. In traditional methods, when healing and balancing the chakras the appropriate stone is normally placed on the chakra (front or back whatever is most comfortable for you) during the exercise. It all depends on the use you programmed into the crystal or stone. Absorb the energy and allow it to work within you and then put the crystal back in its place of storage. Always thank the crystal/stone after an energy transfer. Here's a chart of some stones and crystals that correspond to each chakra:

Chakra	Crystal or Stone
Crown:	Apophyllite, Kunzite, Muscovite, Selenite, Celestite, Purple Sapphire, Moldavite, Purple Jasper, Lepidolite, Citrine, Golden Beryl, Quartz, Clear Tourmaline, Red Serpentine.
Third Eye:	Blue Obsidian, Apophyllite, Sodalite, Royal Sapphire, Azurite, Moldavite, Malachite, Lepidolite, Fluorite, Kunzite, Garnet, Lapis Lazuli, Diamond, Purple Fluorite
Throat:	Lepidolite, Blue Obsidian, Blue Tourmaline, Amber, Azurite, Kunzite, Turquoise, Amethyst, Blue Topaz, Aquamarine
Heart:	Dioptase, Kunzite, Green Sapphire, Rose Quartz, Aventurine, Green Quartz, Chrysocolla, Ruby, Pink Danburite, Variscite, Red Calcite, Watermelon Pink and Green Tourmaline, Rhondonite, Apophyllite, Lepidolite, Morganite
Solar Plexus:	Malachite, Rhodochrosite, Jasper, Tiger's Eye, Golden Beryl, Tourmaline, Citrine, Yellow
Sacral:	Citrine, Blue Jasper, Red Jasper, Orange Carnelian, Topaz
Base:	Azurite, Boji Stone, Bloodstone, Fire Agate, Chrysocolla, Brown Jasper, Smoky Quartz, Obsidian, Golden Yellow Topaz, Hematite, Mahogany Obsidian, Black Tourmaline, Carnelian, Citrine, Tourmaline, Rhondonite, Cuprite, Red Jasper, Smoky Quartz, Cuprite.
To Stimulate a Chakra:	Orange & Red
To Sedate:	Blue & Green
To Elevate:	Violet & Turquoise
To Ground:	Smoky Quartz Crystal used from Crown to Root
Cleansing all chakras:	Amber, Dendritic, Agate, Malachite, Tourmaline, Garnet.

Cleansing lower chakras:	Bloodstone
Alignment:	Boji Stone & Yellow Kunzite
Protecting:	Tourmaline & Garnet
To Open All:	Amber, Dendritic, Agate, Malachite.
Uniting Crown and Heart:	Charoite

Chapter Four
Chakra Divination™ Spreads
Conducting an intuitive reading using the cards and charts

Now that we've discussed the chakras and how they work and we've prepared our crystals and stones, we're now ready to move into the actual process of Chakra Divination™.

I want to take a minute here to discuss the importance of circles in Chakra Divination™. Circles are never ending and represent many different things in our lives. Marriage is often thought of as part of the circle of life, as is the birth of children and death. Not everyone gets married but we all have our circle of friends, our family circle, and so on. I tend to look deeper for the meaning of circles on a metaphysical level. When I do readings for people I see their energy as a circle moving around their waist. This energy may move at a normal pace with nothing affecting it or it may be too fast, too slow or even be stagnant. It might have fluctuations, glitches and waves in addition to the speed of rotation.

The chakras are the same way. When in balance they rotate smoothly at a normal speed and without abnormalities. When they are out of balance they will slow down, speed up or have glitches. Since the shape of the chakras is circular and they rotate in a circular motion and because I see a person's energy as a circular pattern, then it is only fitting that circles are the key element to Chakra Divination™. The patterns you will learn in the card spreads are also circular in nature. When we bring a chakra back into balance we're also doing it by going through a circular process.

In the graphics that show the card layouts, the placement of the card is indicated by a circle. I originally designed the cards as a four inch circular deck but the activity book would have been huge had I used them in this manner. It was more practical to include rectangular cards in this activity book so that it would also be easier for you to handle as you create your own unique deck. And the message that this should be the first presentation of this material was very strong so I'm going with the impression even if it seems weird to me right now. I also felt trimming out eighty-two circular cards may have given you some frustration, and I didn't want that to happen. So, the Chakra Divination™ cards are presented in the activity book as easy to cut out rectangles.

Chakra Divination™ Charts

The Chakra Divination™ charts are used to do a reading for yourself when you need a solution as to why you're feeling blocked. The name of each card is also on the charts so you will refer to the card meanings when interpreting your chart reading.

Chakra Chart: Use this chart when you're not sure which charka you need to work on.
Problem Chart: This chart is used to find the reason why your chakra is out of balance.
Course of Action Chart: This is used to find the action you should take in order to bring your chakra back into balance.
Solution Chart: This is used to find the eventual outcome that you'll achieve when you get your chakra in balance.

How do you use the Problem, Course of Action and Solution charts? There are two ways: with crystals/stones or a pendulum. I prefer crystals or stones so I don't inadvertently look at the chart's text. You should choose the tool that is the most comfortable for you.

Choose the chakra that you feel is blocked based on what you've read so far. If you're not sure, use the crystals or pendulum on the chakra chart first after reading the sample divination reading below. Now, with that chakra in mind, select a crystal or stone of the corresponding color or that you've previously programmed to work with the specific chakra that's out of balance. I'll do a sample reading so you can see how this works. This exercise should be done in a calm, focused, and intuitive manner when you're alone and it's quiet. Turn off your cell phone, unplug your landline and disconnect from instant messaging before you start your reading. If you can avoid interruptions you'll obtain a clearer message.

Sample Chakra Divination™ Chart Reading

I've selected the Solar Plexus Chakra to work on in this example with a Tiger's Eye because that is what feels right for this reading. I connect with my stone and the charts on an intuitive level. I don't want to throw my stone like dice so I close my eyes and rotate the Problem chart in several circles to get the energy of the chart moving in the direction that is most fitting my situation. I silently ask my guides to tell me when to change directions and when to stop spinning the chart. I do this because it's easy for me to memorize what each square on the chart says and I don't want my desires or ego to be a factor in the reading. I also want my guides to assist in the process to give me a clear answer. By moving in alternate directions and in a circular pattern I don't know which way the chart is facing when I lay down my stone. When I feel the chart's in the right position I stop. I use the hand not holding the stone to feel the edges of the chart so I know where it's at. Remember to keep your eyes closed at this point.

Now, holding my closed fist containing the Tiger's Eye on or slightly above the chart, I move it around until I feel the intuitive need to stop. Now I gently place the crystal on the chart and open my eyes. My stone is inside the Low Vitality box. Had the stone been on a line with a portion of the stone inside more than one box, I would consider the information in all of the boxes it touches. If a larger portion of the stone is in one box and less in another, then the box that contains the majority of the stone will be the predominant factor to consider in the reading. However, don't rule out the information in the box that contains less of the stone because sometimes we have multiple reasons that a chakra is out of balance.

After writing down the information from the Chakra chart, I now repeat all of my prior actions with the Course of Action chart. This time my stone is lying on the box that says Greater Good. And lastly I do the same with the Solution chart and the stone is in the box that says Energized.

So what does this mean? To me, the chakra chart reading is showing me that the reason my solar plexus chakra is out of balance is because I'm doing too much which is resulting in a feeling of low vitality. The way I can resolve this and bring my solar plexus chakra back into balance is to let go of that which doesn't serve my greater good as indicated by the Course of Action chart. These would be the things in my life that are taking a lot of energy but are not giving me much back in return. As I let them go I will find that I have time to get more rest because I will have less on my plate to cause stress in my daily activities. This action on my part will bring about an abundance of energy in my life and allow new things to come to me as indicated by the Solution chart.

You can use this same process with a pendulum. Instead of moving the charts in circles before placing the crystal, simply begin by focusing on your pendulum and asking it to circle as it searches for the correct reason within the chart and intending it to stop on the most appropriate response. Don't look at the chart but instead give all of your attention to the pendulum. This is to prevent your own thoughts and ego from interfering with the reading. The pendulum will begin to swing in a wide circular or back and forth motion. When it is over the box that is the most appropriate response for the chakra you've chosen to balance, it will stop moving completely or the motion will become so small that it does not move outside of the square. Repeat this same process on the Course of Action and Solution charts and then interpret your results using the meanings included in this book.

When doing this exercise it is important to accept the results as you receive them. Sometimes you'll have to look deeper at what you're seeing, past what you may think the initial meaning is, in order to get to the root and exact cause of the blockage. For instance, what if I'd gotten the box that says "Insecurity"? I could have let my ego and doubt invade the reading by saying, "I am *not* insecure!" This will give me an inaccurate result because I'm denying that insecurity is affecting me. However, if I look deeper I might see that I am insecure about something in my life. By accepting what the reading is saying and trying to look deeper for the problem, then it will be easier for me to bring myself back into balance following the Course of Action to obtain the Solution.

Remember that the cards and charts are just a tool. Once you've done a reading on yourself you must follow through with the guidance offered by the cards, charts and your own intuition in order to see a change in your life that will bring balance to your chakras. I always suggest writing down your readings in the *Chakra Divination™ Ultimate Balance Journal* so you can keep up with what you're working on now and what areas you've worked on in the past. This way you can be assured that you're following though on the readings that you're doing to help center yourself and balance your chakras. Writing things down is always a good idea because memory may not serve you as well and you may forget details.

There are four different spreads used in Chakra Divination™ with one spread having two options. In the section below I'm going to explain how to lay out the cards for each of these spreads and how to read the lay of each spread. Remember that you should always use your intuition and connection to the cards while shuffling and dealing each spread.

For each of these spreads the first thing that you will do is divide your cards into the four suits. The first will be all of the Chakra cards, the second all of the Problem cards, the third all of the Course of Action cards and the fourth the Solution cards. Now, shuffle each suit separately. Start with your Chakra cards and once you feel that the cards are mixed correctly then stop and lay them down. You may also cut the cards, if you so desire, in between or after shuffling. Once complete, leave them in a stack and move on to the next suit, the Problem cards. Do the same thing, shuffle and cut until it feels right, restack and then do the remaining two suits. When all of the cards have been shuffled and/or cut you're ready to start the spread you've chosen.

Four Card Chakra Spread

This spread is designed to give you a quick answer when you know which chakra is out of balance. Within this spread there are two spread options, shown in the following graphics, for laying out the cards. After shuffling all the card suits and placing them in four different stacks, pick up the Chakra cards to choose the appropriate card for the chakra you want to work on and lay in it the number one position of the option you're using.

If you're not sure which chakra is out of balance, hold the Chakra cards face down in your hand, focus with the intention that the appropriate card will feel drawn to you, shuffle and then choose a card and place it in the number one position. Next, choose the top card from the shuffled Problem cards and lay it in the number two position. If you feel you need to shuffle again before choosing the card, do so now. This card will tell you the problem, as it currently is, within the chakra indicated by the card you just placed in the number one position. Now, take the top card from the Course of Action cards and place it in the number three position. This is what you need to do in order to reach a Solution and get the chakra back into balance. Choose the top card from the Solution suit and put it in the number four position. Read what each card says and then follow through with the Course of Action in your life in order to reach the given Solution.

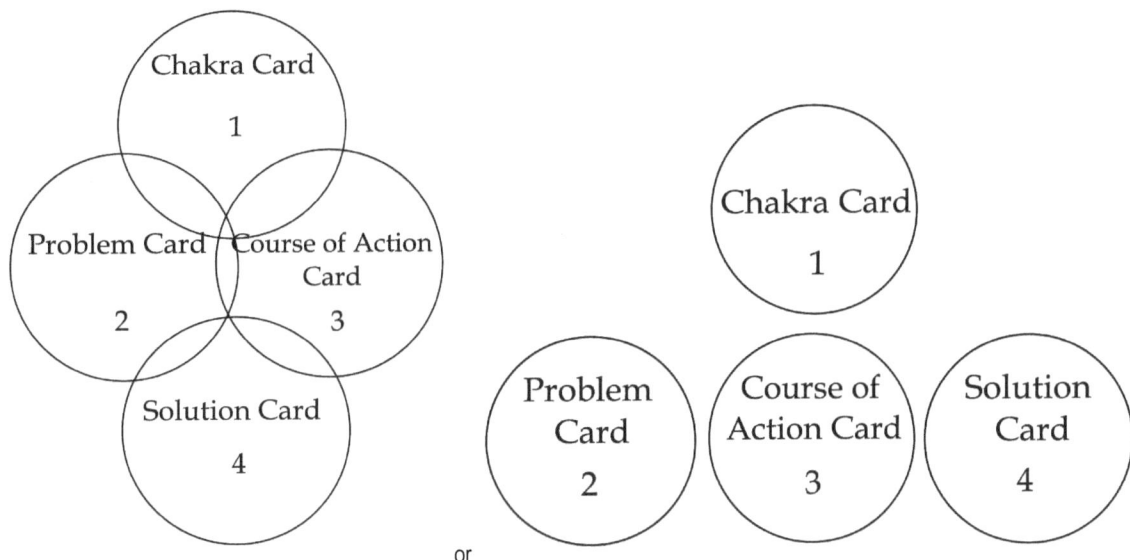

or

Lotus Petal Spread

To look deeper into one chakra you'll do what I call the Lotus Petal Spread. The lotus flower is often associated with the chakras because it symbolizes emergence from darkness into the light. In this spread you have six points that are connected to the Chakra card which is placed in the center of the spread. Here's what you do. After shuffling you'll choose the Chakra card for the chakra that you want to investigate. Lay this card in the center. Now choose two Problem cards and put them in positions two and five as shown in the graphic. Next you'll choose two Course of Action cards and put them in positions three and six. Then do the same thing for the Solution cards and lay them in positions four and seven.

Begin by examining the Problem cards. How do they relate to the chakra? Do they relate to each other? These two cards will identify the two most important problems or issues happening within the chakra. Make sure you examine what this says intently because sometimes looking at the top layer of a problem isn't really going to resolve it. You have to look deeper and seek a greater understanding. Also, you may be in denial about the problem indicated by the card and decide that you need to redo the layout. Don't be so quick to push the initial draw aside. Look closer and see what you find. Once you feel connected to the problems at hand move to the Course of Action cards for each situation. This is how you're going to start to balance the chakra. Don't forget to look truthfully within yourself. If you follow this Course of Action you will reach the indicated Solution. Now examine the Solution cards you drew. This is what you can expect as a reward and balance for delving deeper into the problem with this chakra.

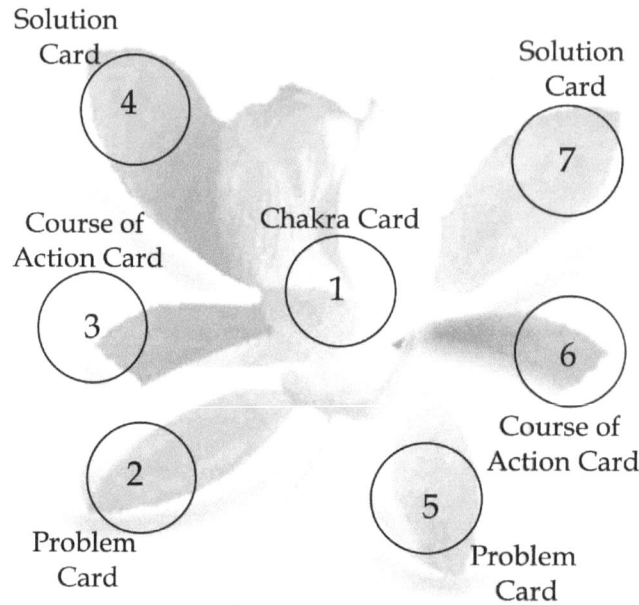

Full Chakra Spread

In this spread you will examine the Problem, Course of Action and Solution for each of the seven chakras. I find it helpful to lay this spread with the cards face down, and then as I turn the cards over, I only reveal one column at a time starting with the Chakra card and ending with the Solution card. Once I understand what the first row is telling me about the chakra, I move to the next Chakra card in row two and so forth until I've examined the entire spread.

First separate and cut each of the four suits. Shuffle and lay all seven Chakra cards in row one. Next shuffle and lay seven Problem cards in row two, seven Course of Action cards in row three and seven Solution cards in row four. Put the remaining cards aside.

Begin by turning over the first Chakra card, then the first Problem card, the first Course of Action card and the first Solution card. You now have one column revealed. Study this column until you have a good idea of how to proceed in balancing this chakra. Continue to row two and so forth until you've examined the entire layout and have a Problem, Course of Action and Solution for each chakra.

This spread contains a lot of valuable information. I suggest you do it at a time when you can put your entire focus into this reading; a time when you'll be uninterrupted. I would also suggest writing down the results that you receive as you're analyzing each column. You might include notes to yourself about your initial feelings and thoughts regarding each column. This is an extra step but as you try to balance your chakras you will want to refer back to the reading and the chart to make sure you're staying on track.

Chakra Divination™ Cards & Charts Activity Book

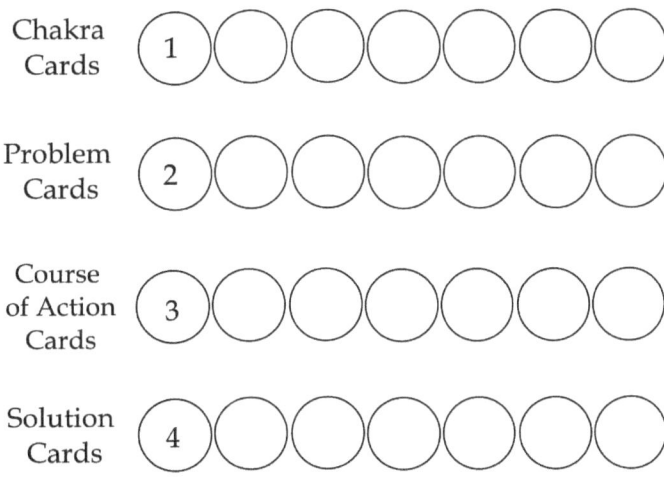

The Chakra Circle Spread

This final spread is the most complex and detailed of all of the spreads. It will give you the foundation to bring balance to each chakra individually. It will also provide an ultimate overall change in your whole person if you follow the advice given in the cards. You will build on the foundation and grow from there through resolving the problems associated with each chakra. If you feel that one or more of your chakras are already in balance then you'd probably want to go with the Lotus Petal Spread or a Four Card Spread on the chakras that feel out of balance.

This spread is primarily for use when you feel that there is something a little off with all of your chakras and/or you want to deepen your spirituality by doing chakra work. It gives you a foundation to grow on and an Ultimate Change to reach toward to obtain Ultimate Balance. As with the other spreads, I suggest that you write the results down so you can refer back to it at a later date to make sure you're staying on the right track as shown through the reading.

To do this spread you're going to build outward and then work inward. Study the following layout prior to beginning so you'll understand the spread before actually attempting it. The more times you use this spread the easier it is to remember. Choose a table where you can lay the cards out because this spread requires a lot of space. Start by shuffling all of the four card suits separately. You can also choose to shuffle again any time you feel the need during the drawing and laying of this spread (or any of the Chakra Divination™ spreads). Remember to always trust your intuition because it is the primary principal in this method. Once you've shuffled each suit place it in its own pile. Pick up the Chakra cards and deal them in an even circle laying them face down.

Now you're ready to deal the Problem, Course of Action and Solution cards. Lay them in a triangular pattern around each Chakra card, also face down. Pick up the Problem cards and deal from the top, placing one card on the left side of the area where you'll build your triangle. Lay one Problem card for each of the chakras. Do the same thing with the Course of Action card, laying it to the right beside the Problem card. Give each Chakra card one Course of Action card. To finish building your triangle, lay one Solution card at the top of the triangle above the Problem and Course of Action cards. Give one Solution card to each Chakra card.

You've built outward so now its time to work on the interior. This is where you lay your foundation cards. Pick up your remaining Course of Action cards and reshuffle and cut them until you feel that they are ready. Lay down three Course of Action cards, creating a triangle. These are the paths you will take for overall spiritual growth and chakra balance.

Lay down the Course of Action cards and pick up the remaining Solution cards. Shuffle them until they feel like they are in the correct order. Place the top card between the triangle created by the foundation Course of Action cards. This is the Ultimate Change that will happen to you once your chakras are balanced. This spread can also be laid out in reverse if you feel the need to draw and lay down the interior cards before the outside cards. This is totally fine and you should always follow your intuition during Chakra Divination™.

To read this layout, always start by turning over one Chakra card and then the three cards in the triangle for that chakra in the exterior circle. You want to save the four Course of Action cards and the one Ultimate Change card in the interior section of the spread until the end of the reading even if you laid them down first. Go through this same procedure with all the Chakra cards in the outer circle. Once this process is complete, then move to the interior triangle. You will turn over the Course of Action foundation cards first. These are the three things that you must do to succeed in moving along your spiritual path and opening your chakras so that you will have a balanced fulfilling life. Now, turn over the Ultimate Change card. This is what you will achieve when you have balanced all of your chakras. This is your ultimate reward for your hard work.

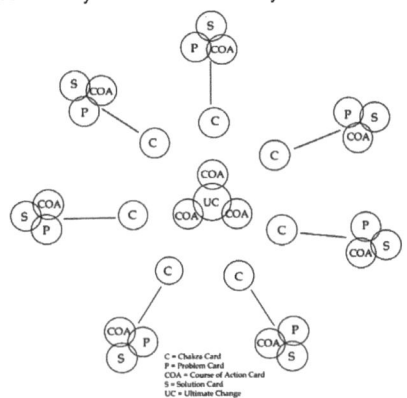

C = Chakra Card
P = Problem Card
COA = Course of Action Card
S = Solution Card
UC = Ultimate Change

15

Chapter Five
Chakra Divination™ Card Meaning
Bring balance to the chakras

With each of the Chakra cards, the **In The Spread** meanings apply whether you've randomly selected the chakra to work on or have chosen it with purpose. The title of each card is also found on the charts. While I have used the word *card* in the meanings, they apply to both chart and card readings.

The Chakra Cards

Crown Chakra – The Seventh Chakra is located at the top of your head and associated with the colors violet, purple and white. It is the main energy center that connects you to the higher realms, increases spiritual awareness and your ability to *know*. It is your connection to God and the Universe. Your union with the Divine is of utmost importance when drawing this card, bringing inner wisdom, spiritual growth and a heightened state of enlightenment. It is your spiritual connection to divine consciousness, the source of God's white light and indicates your right to aspire to great heights on many levels. **In The Spread:** When you draw the **Crown Chakra**, now is the time to get in touch with your spirituality and liberate yourself from the confines of the Earthly realm by seeking Universal Knowledge. Connection with your own spirituality is needed now. Divine guidance is waiting for you to take the initial step, to ask for help in balancing your spiritual connections within yourself and the Universe. You have an innate knowledge of, and connection with, the Universe and the spiritual realms. Embrace your own divinity, allow the energy of the **Crown Chakra** to open and connect you with your true self, which is pure spiritual energy. When you unite with the Divine, you will feel the powerful rotations of the chakra as a **Lightness of Being** as it spins faster. Silence allows an even deeper bond to Universal Energy. Take time to immerse yourself in, and listen intently to, silence. Allow your inner self to become one with the Higher Realms, resulting in the fulfillment of your true destiny and ultimate inner peace and happiness.

Third Eye Chakra - The Sixth Chakra is located in the forehead between the eyes and is associated with the color indigo. It gives you the ability to look up into the spiritual realms. It is essential in the development of psychic abilities, trusting intuition and understanding insights. It is a key factor in self-realization and releasing hidden or negative thoughts that may be holding you back from your fullest potential. It provides a means to see into other dimensions and an understanding of what you're seeing. It's associated with imagination, dreaming and all things metaphysical. **In The Spread:** It is important to embrace your own psychic abilities, to accept them for what they are and allow them to grow within you. It doesn't matter what others think, it is your own self-realization of your abilities that is important now. To further your own spiritual growth, you must accept all parts of yourself. Only in this way will you bring balance to the **Third Eye Chakra**. Ignoring or denying your abilities and intuition will only cause further blocks within the chakra. Fear should be released now, completely erased, to gain clear sight, feel grounded and calm your mind. You cannot see through that which you fear. Pay attention to anything that stands out to you as odd or different because these may offer a new awareness. Spirit surrounds you, aiding you in balancing this chakra. Listen and accept the insights you are given, leaving doubt behind.

Throat Chakra - The Fifth Chakra is located in the throat region and is associated with the color blue. It represents the truthful self and the expression of your beliefs. The **Throat Chakra** is the free expression of the soul's inner truth. It is very important in trusting yourself and others. Creativity, organization and the ability to plan stems from a balanced throat chakra. The **Throat Chakra** is vital in transforming the self, making changes and connecting to inner truth. **In The Spread:** Now is the time to look truthfully at your inner self, the real you. Do you speak the truth or do you tell white lies or big flat-out lies? Telling a lie, whether big or small is blocking the soul's right to free expression. Not only are you blocking your inner light from shining through, you are clouding that light, diminishing its strength with your untruths. Drawing the **Throat Chakra** is notice that you must free yourself from everything that isn't truth. Look at yourself for whom and what you are, and accept what you find as your real nature, your soul's essence, for in doing so, you bring balance and light to yourself. Once you have found your balance in truth, your creativity will also shine. You'll naturally become more organized and will be able to express yourself without hesitation. This is a card of self-transformation. It suggests a time of change, of forward movement and growth on a spiritual level.

Heart Chakra – The Fourth Chakra is located in the center of your chest and associated with the color green. It represents the ability to give and receive love, to give and accept forgiveness and compassion. It affects self-control and acceptance of your spirituality on every level. All relationships are affected by the **Heart Chakra**. It is the storage center of all of your emotional experiences. **In The Spread:** Drawing the **Heart Chakra** is an indication that your emotions, especially those concerning loving yourself and others, is out of balance. In order to bring balance back to this chakra you must look inside and see if you really, truly love yourself. For without loving yourself, you can't give true love to others. If you find that you don't love yourself as you should, then drawing this card is indicative that it is time to forgive yourself, accept yourself and truly love the glorious soul that you are. This is the time to forgive those who have wronged you in the past, to open yourself to freely accept love and compassion from others and to give that same love and compassion in return. By being sympathetic to others and having empathy for people going through difficult times, you not only bring balance to this chakra but you learn to love yourself even more. This is a card of emotional self-acceptance and hope.

Solar Plexus Chakra - The Third Chakra is located in the stomach area right above the navel and is associated with the color yellow. It affects feelings of personal power, self esteem, self-confidence, ego, humor and the ability to think clearly. It is the center of our emotions, a power center that houses our inner drive. While the **Heart Chakra** is the storage center for your emotions, the **Solar Plexus Chakra** is the center from which your emotions originate. **In The Spread:** This is your personal power center. Drawing the **Solar Plexus Chakra** card indicates that you need to take the bull by the horns. This is the time to follow your gut instincts, take risks and make decisions. Take a stand, be a leader, not a follower. If you're an overachiever who is overflowing with personal power, vitality and your ego matches a high level of assertiveness, now is the time to pull back some and relax. Too much or to little when it comes to the **Solar Plexus Chakra** will keep it out of balance and have you slinking behind the crowd or at the front lines charging ahead. While it's fine to take either of these positions, when you only take one or the other, you never sit in middle ground and this is where balance is found. Don't overdo, but don't neglect your personal power either. When this chakra is in balance you'll find that your vitality soars, you are more perceptive and have powerful insights which isn't available to you during times of imbalance. By finding balance you will have positive self-esteem and self-confidence without being overbearing.

Sacral Chakra - The Second or Spleen Chakra is located in the lower abdomen right below the navel, is associated with the color orange and affects our ability to feel. It is indicative of how we interact in social situations including intimate relationships. It is the center of our feelings. It is also important to our sexual and reproductive selves. **In The Spread:** The **Sacral Chakra** drawn in the spread means that you need to work on your feelings. If this chakra is rotating too slowly you may feel that nothing ever goes right, as if you're blocked but don't know why. Your creativity may be at an all time low and you may be having problems getting along with others. You feel stuck, static and have low confidence. You may avoid social situations simply because you feel as if you don't fit in. When you bring balance to this chakra it's as if you've turned over a new leaf. Your confidence and creativity soars, you feel open and nothing bothers you. Problems roll right off of you like water rolls off of a duck's back. You are able to flow with situations as they happen in your life instead of feeling blocked at every turn. You're full of grace and acceptance. The **Sacral Chakra** is also directly related to how you feel about yourself sexually. If you're afraid of intimacy and pleasure, if warm gestures from others make you uncomfortable (even if they aren't sexual in nature) then you are out of balance in this chakra and need to take immediate corrective action so that you'll be able to experience warmth, pleasure and intimacy.

Root/Base Chakra - The First Chakra is located at the base of the spine near the tailbone and is associated with the color red. It is our ability to survive. It grounds us in the physical and material world. It contains the eight cells that hold all the knowledge of creation. It is your ability to stand up for yourself, personal feelings of security and the way you relate to the internal instinct to survive. **In The Spread:** You are human; therefore, you're an animal with survival instincts. Drawing the **Root/Base Chakra** is an indication that you need to work on your foundation, the basic connections between mind, body and spirit. When the foundation isn't solid, the house can't stand but will crumble in time. It is the same with you. If you don't have a solid foundation, you will crack under pressure; you will not feel grounded to the Earth. You may feel as if you're losing your identity, that you aren't connected to your body, your needs or desires. When the foundation is firm and strong you will be more self-sufficient, more stable in your emotions and will feel a connection to everything around you. You will trust more because you're grounded within yourself and will be ready to build upon your own inner strength.

The Problem Cards

Absentminded – You can't express yourself clearly. You're frequently forgetful and easily distracted. You often daydream and are inattentive to your surroundings. It's easier to tune people out then to deal with the situations in your life. There is a lack of concentration. In conversation you flitter from one topic to another and may not make sense to the person you're talking too. **In The Spread:** Now is the time to pay more attention to the world around you and make a concentrated effort to focus more on the details of your life. You need to reduce stress because it can be a detrimental factor that causes absentmindedness. Drawing **Absentminded** is indicative that you need to bring the self back to center because the energy of the chakra you're working on is moving in slow rotation. You can't interact with others and live your life if you're constantly in a state of forgetfulness or living in a fantasy world of daydreams. Ground yourself to the Earth, reconnect to your soul energy by making a purposeful effort to be attentive and focused.

Anger – Aggression and assertiveness abounds in your daily life. How is anger projecting through your actions? Do you have an explosive temper, a short fuse, or a mean streak? If you do, then the root cause of these things is anger. **In The Spread:** While it's natural to lose your temper now and again, when **Anger** shows up in a spread, it's indicative of a deeper emotional trauma. Anger is based in fear. In order to bring balance back to the chakra you're working on, you have to release all anger, just let it go completely. Before you can do that, you need to realize the true reason for the anger. If you go through life mad at the world, there's a reason for this. When anger gets the best of you, then you are usually trying to force your will on another and aren't getting your way, or, you have put your trust in someone who has hurt you. Anger can grow until it takes over your life and that's no way to live. Look for the root cause of your anger, face it, acknowledge it and then let it go. If you need to be angry, then be angry, if you need to cry over the reason you're angry, then cry, but ultimately in the end you have to let the angry feelings go. Embracing anger and feeding it is only hurting you. While you can't do anything about how others treat you, you can treat yourself well and let go of ill feelings. Remember, we all have our own life lessons to learn and anger can hold us back from growing because it blocks you, it sits inside you and festers until you explode or until it eats away at you, leaving you as a shell of what you could be in this lifetime. It's not worth it. This card means it's time to look for hidden anger and hostility and release it.

Anxiety – When you're anxious, nothing will go right for you. You worry about every little thing, you have mood swings, you may bite your fingernails, have nervous habits, even develop a twitch. You may often take your anxiety out on those you love the most because you're short tempered. **In The Spread:** You're surrounded by negativity. You may be in a negative environment or situation; you're blocked by your surroundings or the situation itself, which intensifies the anxious feelings. Physically remove yourself from the environment/situation to allow positivity to come though. If your job is having an ill effect on you, causing high stress and anxiety, look for a new job. Life is too short to be constantly worried about or obsessed over little things that happen in your life. But before you up and move to a different place for a new job, make sure that you're not causing yourself anxiety when there isn't a reason for it. If you tend to blow things out of proportion, then decide if the anxiety is really necessary or if you are dramatizing the situation, making it more than it is. Take a good hard look at how you're reacting to situations and decide if you're being overly anxious when there's not a reason for it. If you are, then let go of this emotion immediately. Anxiety has a negative effect on your chakra energy.

Avoidance – Are you ignoring important events, hiding away from life or laying low just so you don't have to deal with life? Do you prefer to steer clear of difficult or uncomfortable situations? If you don't have to deal with it, then maybe it'll just go away, right? **In The Spread:** Drawing the **Avoidance** card is a clear sign that you need to start facing situations head on. It indicates that you're guarding yourself and your emotions and often this is out of fear. Take a look at what you're really afraid of that is causing you to divert your attention elsewhere. Do you feel as if you don't fit in, that people will make fun of you or that you will not live up to the expectations that others have placed upon you? Take some time to think about why you're avoiding things; do you expect too much of yourself and feel you will not meet your own expectations? Avoidance will keep your chakras out of balance because it is a negative action, one that can lower your self-esteem unless you determine the real reason why you're evading people and events in your life. Avoidance is a means of escape. When you feel the need to vanish and hide it's because you're not comfortable with yourself or have fear. No matter what your current situation, facing it will bring balance to your chakra and a sense of personal liberation.

Barrier – Obstacles stand in your way. You cannot grow spiritually or emotionally because the way is not clear. You are at an impasse and don't know which way to turn. **In The Spread:** When **Barrier** shows in the spread, this is an indication that you must not take the quick way out. Do not try to go around the obstacles that are blocking your path and hindering your spiritual growth. Instead, figure out what they are and take steps to remove them. This is a time for calm reasoning. Look at all sides of the situation to determine the cause of the barrier and the best way to remove it. In relationships with others, you may have to change your way of thinking to avoid arguments or smooth out tension that is between you and the other person. Spiritually, are you putting barriers up against yourself? Are you trying too hard when it comes to understanding your psychic abilities or spiritual growth instead of just letting it happen naturally? **Barrier** can bring the energy in your chakras to a standstill, to a slow rotation that is barely moving until you determine the cause and make a plan to remove barriers from your path.

Chaos – Your world just went crazy. Chaos throws your life into a spin and it feels as if nothing is going right. Everything is blown way out of proportion; the foundation and structure of your life just fell apart. Everything that could go wrong is going wrong and you feel helpless to stop it. **In The Spread:** When you draw **Chaos** in the spread this is a sign that you need to take a step back and look at what's happening as a stranger looking in. By taking an impartial point of view you will notice cause and effect, you will be able to make assessments that you may have missed while you're stuck in the middle of the chaos going on in your life. Now is the time to put emotions on the back burner, get the facts straight and use logical and critical thinking to solve problems with ease. Drawing **Chaos** is an indication that you must rise above the pandemonium going on around you to see the situation clearly. This is the prime objective in bringing balance back to the chakra in question.

Confusion – This is a time of bewilderment and uncertainty. You don't know which choice to make, which way to turn or who you can trust. The confusion is within you because you're not clear and focused within your own mind. **In The Spread:** You now have several choices in front of you and each one could tilt the energy of the chakras in either direction. If you're not sure what decision is the right one based on your situation then make a list and look at the possible effects of each choice. Does your confusion stem from a relationship with someone else? Then maybe you need to have a discussion with them prior to making your choice. Always remember that in order to bring balance to your own chakra energy you must do what feels right for you, not what someone else wants you to do. If you are uncomfortable with a potential decision, then don't let confusion cloud your judgment. Now is the time to reflect upon your own spirituality. You may not have the same belief system as anyone else on this planet but if that belief system feels right to you, than it is. Why? Because we all have different spiritual pathways to follow and lessons to learn; what is right for one may not be right for another. Only you know your place in this world and the path you must take. Following your own convictions will bring balance and harmony to your chakras.

Detachment – You feel indifferent and uninvolved in your life. In other words, you could care less about the world around you or your role in it. You may find fault with others but see no fault in yourself. You push others away even when they are trying to offer assistance. **In The Spread:** The **Detachment** card is an indication that you are retreating from life. You may see yourself as a victim. You are separated from your core self, from your energy sources. You are on autopilot and just going through the motions. People may see you as superficial and aloof, conceited or vain. You think others are out to get you when in fact the problem lies within you. Now is the time to take an active role in your life. Instead of hiding away and showing no interest, you must look objectively at your feelings, your deep emotions and find balance within your core being in order to bring stability to your chakra energy.

Doubt – This is an indication that you do not believe, you're puzzled and uncertain. You are skeptical and undecided about the situation. You tend to distrust yourself, others and may be involved in questionable situations and circumstances. **In The Spread:** Do you doubt your abilities, your spiritual path or the lessons placed before you? The pathway is clear except for your own reservations. When you cast doubt aside and make a definite decision you will bring balance to the chakra. Do not be hasty in this decision because doubt appears for a reason and can serve as protection from negative forces. When **Doubt** is drawn in the spread it is also an indication that you need to take the time to make sure you are comfortable with the situations you are in, that any other people involved have answered your questions and seem honest in their interactions with you. Drawing **Doubt** is also indicative of internal disbelief in your true nature and inner self.

Fear – An overwhelming emotion. You are afraid because you sense danger or a threat to your person, whether it's physical or emotional. Spiritually you may be frightened to move from one level to the other because you do not know what lies beyond. **In The Spread: Fear** in the spread is an indication that you are holding back because you are unsure of what will happen if you take a leap of faith spiritually. When you are afraid of the unknown you are limiting the amount of spiritual growth you can achieve. This is a negative emotion that can stop your chakra energy from having any motion at all. Fear has no place in our lives unless your life is being physically threatened and then it's only human nature to be afraid. To live daily in a state of fear, whether it's fear of change, fear of the unknown or phobias that you are clinging too can only do your energy harm. Fear holds you back, it pulls you down and it can turn an outgoing carefree person into a quiet hermit who never leaves the house. Facing your fears allows you to acknowledge that they are your own creation and lets you release them, freeing you from their negative energy.

Foreboding - Doom and gloom abounds. You feel a sense of dread, as if something bad is about to happen at any minute, but you aren't sure what it is. **In The Spread:** When **Foreboding** is drawn in the spread it is a message to you that all is not as it appears. Examine the chakra that you are working on. If it is a lower chakra then its energy is at an all time low and you will want to work on balance through energizing the chakra, by bringing positivity into your life instead if having a deep seated sense of apprehension on a daily basis. If the chakra you're working on is in the upper levels then the energy is probably rotating quickly, helping you attune to some outside force that is about to act upon you. When the upper level chakras are involved, so are your psychic senses and connectivity to the Universe. In this case the sense of foreboding isn't a daily occurrence you're living with but a premonition of something that is about to happen. Take note and pay attention to what is going on around you.

Guilt – When you feel responsible for yourself and everyone around you, then guilt can be an overwhelming emotion. When anything bad happens you feel it is your fault, that you are the guilty party when in fact you may not be. You may feel that you're a miserable failure, that you've dishonored yourself or someone else or that you are at fault. You are ashamed of things you have done that you know doesn't serve your **Greater Good** and feel the need to make it right. **In The Spread: Guilt** in the spread is a sign that your self esteem is low, that your chakras are very out of balance and that you're taking on responsibility and pressures that you do not own. Let others take responsibility for their actions. You cannot feel guilty for that which you have not done. Don't worry that you have done something wrong in the eyes of others, for the only eyes that you need to worry about are the eyes of God. If you know in your heart that you are truly doing the best you can in life, then guilt will not be a part of it. If you have indeed done something shameful, something that you know is wrong, now is the time to either accept it as a lesson learned or fix it by telling the truth and accepting whatever consequences go along with that truth. You've heard the old saying that the truth will set you free? It does, and not only that, it will bring balance within your chakras.

Hatred – In today's world hatred is everywhere, but that doesn't mean you have to embrace it too. Envy, jealousy, loathing, disgust; these go hand in hand with hatred. Nothing good ever comes out of this extremely negative emotion. **In The Spread:** When hatred comes up in the spread, you really have to do some soul searching to bring balance to the affected chakra. Maybe you don't think you have hatred within you, maybe it's hidden so deep that you deny it even to yourself. In order to bring balance to the energy of the chakra you're working on, you must look deeply within yourself and at your actions. Are you jealous of others? Do you envy what they have? Do some people simply disgust you because you feel they are beneath you? Acting like this is a form of hatred. Do you hate yourself, your family or your boss? In order to release hatred from your life you must find the initiating action that caused you to feel hatred in the first place. Once you've found the root cause, analyze it. Is the hatred within you because someone else taught you to hate? Or is it there because of something you experienced first hand. Holding onto hatred will destroy you; it can be all consuming, until you're only a shell of yourself because you're so addicted to the hatred you're feeling. And yes, hatred is an addiction, one that must be overcome before you can bring balance to the chakra. When this is accomplished, peace and **Lightness of Being** will replace the dark, cold, angry feelings of hatred.

Illness – Encompassing health problems, physical aches and pains. You have feelings outside of the normal realm of healthy consciousness. Illness is not only related to physical and mental health but you can be spiritually ill as well. **In The Spread:** The **Illness** card drawn during a reading is telling you to sit up and take notice of your mind, body and spirit. While you may not be physically ill at this point in time, illness may be coming toward you. There may be negative energies gathering around you, waiting to strike. This is the time to make sure you're eating right, are using the sanitizing wipes that are out in public places to clean your shopping carts and are drinking plenty of fluids, even if you're not sick. If you do come down with a cold or some other health issue, visualize it melting from you, leaving you robust and well. Spiritually, look for illness within your energy fields. You will feel off center and out of balance in more than one chakra. Other people, typically called energy vampires, are attached to your energy source; draining you and making you feel worn out, as if you're coming down with a bug when it's not a physical illness at all. Use creative visualization to remove attachments these people have placed upon you, disconnecting them from your energy centers. Taking extra care of yourself now will center the chakras and make you feel better on many different levels.

Lethargy – You're tired, depressed, exhausted and indifferent to the world around you. Sleep sounds really good right about now, even though you may have just woken up. People may think of you as lazy, but you disagree. You feel stuck in life, with no purpose or drive. If the lethargy has gone on for a while, you may have grown accustomed to it and are now comfortable with being miserable. Your get up and go feels like it got up and went and you just can't find it anymore. Lethargy can lead to depression so the sooner you can snap out of it the better. **In The Spread:** When **Lethargy** is drawn in the spread, now is the time to take action. You may not feel like you can make a change right now but in order to achieve balance you must pull yourself up out of the mire, shake yourself off and get going again. Staying in the same place and in the same mindset will keep your chakra energy in the same rotation. You must make a change. Even if you're only able to take baby steps, they are a sign of forward motion. You aren't going to get out of this slump until you make an effort. With **Lethargy** in the spread, it's indicative that it may be tough going for a while. You'll have to do things that you initially don't feel are worthwhile but as you increase your efforts you will see positive results.

Low vitality – Your concentration, creativity and energy levels are at a low point. You can't think straight and want to sleep all the time; you have ambition but lack the drive to achieve your goals. You may feel like you don't even have the energy to last through the day. You've lost your zest for life, not out of disinterest, but because of low energy. **In The Spread:** When you draw **Low Vitality** in the spread, this is a wakeup call. Now is the time to bring focus to your life and energize your chakras. Your joy of life is being covered by negative influences, thus causing you to feel out of sorts. It is important that you add invigorating exercises to your schedule; get out and about and change your environment. Just seeing new places, people and things can invigorate you. If your daily routine consists of staying home all day, then leave the house. If you work outside the home, then take a different route to work every day. When you're at home, take a walk, go to the park, do something other than just sitting in front of the television set. To counteract **Low Vitality** you have to physically move and give yourself different high energy experiences even when you don't feel like doing them. Go swimming, join a choir, do anything that you can to add liveliness to your life.

Memories – Living in the past, lack of trust and stagnation. When you're only looking backward at what could have been instead of looking forward at what is to be, you can drain your energy centers. **In The Spread:** To remember is a beautiful thing. Our memories are a part of us that we can look back upon with joy, love and bittersweet happiness. The problem arises when you are constantly living in the past. When you no longer plan for the future or have dreams and goals that you're aiming for, but instead you're staying firmly seated in what you've accomplished in the past or what previously happened between you and others, then you're not living life to the fullest and there is no potential for balance and growth in the chakras. Living in the past is a negative trait which will not only make you unappealing to others but is one that will keep your chakras at low energy rotations. Look ahead to the future and allow good things to come into your life. While you'll never forget, now is the time to allow memories to be what they truly are, past experiences that you can look back upon, not events that you constantly relive in current times. Dwelling on the past prevents you from having experiences that will create new memories because you're too absorbed in what came before.

Nonbeliever – Show me proof and I'll believe it. That's your frame of mind. You have a hard time believing anything that you can't see with your own two eyes. If you haven't experienced it, then it must not exist. You may or may not ridicule people with different beliefs than yourself. It is instinctive for you to question everything before you will say whether you believe in it or not. You're very skeptical and have few things that you believe in. **In The Spread:** When the **Nonbeliever** card comes up in a spread it's because you have been questioning your faith, your spirituality or your ideals and morals. You feel out of focus, off center and uncertain. The chakras are unbalanced and in dire need of being brought back to a positive equilibrium so that you can make decisions and move forward. If being a nonbeliever is a personality trait for you, then now is the time to determine why you have a hard time believing in things. Is it because you were lied to in the past or were you brought up with nonbeliever parents? Take time to dig deeply into your inner self to find the root cause of this problem. Until you ferret it out and address it, the chakras will remain out of balance.

Obsessive – You're thinking about one thing excessively, you're preoccupied with a situation and it turns over and over in your mind, letting you think of little else. **In The Spread:** Setting goals and striving ahead is a great thing to do in life. When you fixate on one particular situation, thing or person, and allow no room for anything else in your mind, then you're obsessed and your chakra energy reflects this as a stagnated rotation. You may feel hyper and energetic but at the chakra level you're moving slowly because you can't seem to wrap your mind around anything but the thing you're obsessing over. You probably sound like a broken record to others. Drawing **Obsessive** in the spread means it's time to break free of this mindset. Let go of these controlling thoughts. Have you heard the saying if you love something set it free and if it is yours it'll come back to you? Well, that applies here. When you obsess over something or someone you're stuck in a pattern of negative thinking. By letting it go, you are allowing yourself growth and if that thing you were so obsessed over is truly supposed to be yours, it'll come to you when you least expect it.

Pride – Are you egotistical, petty and hold yourself in high regard? Do you have an unreasonable amount of self-esteem and feel that you are more important than anyone else on the planet? Do you guard your possessions as if they matter more than the soul? Are you snobbish and have contempt for those around you, thinking you're much better than they are? Do you expect affection and attention from others but never give the same back in return? Then you, my friend, are letting pride get in the way of your spiritual growth. **In The Spread:** Okay, so maybe you're not trying to grow spiritually. Or at least you think that right now because you're unable to see the root of your problem because you put yourself so high above others and the world in your mind's eye. You look upon yourself as a king sitting upon a throne in the clouds, looking down upon mankind and the Earth. Don't get angry reading this, facing the truth is difficult but face it you must. Now is the time to get grounded again, to give up the prideful thoughts and the sense of entitlement. You are not superior to everyone else. Sure, you may have lots of money, live in a nice house, have a college degree; you may have more things than other people but those are just material possessions and when you are too prideful, you're interfering with your spiritual growth. Overcoming a prideful nature may be a life lesson for you. Once you become less arrogant and understand that you are a spiritual entity that is on the Earth plane to learn life lessons just like everyone else, than you will begin to bring balance to your chakra.

Recklessness – This card is indicative of extreme behavior. You don't care about consequences but instead act in a careless and brash manner. You may get a rush of excitement from living on the edge, taking risks and acting like a daredevil. Hasty, inattentive, indiscrete and inconsiderate behavior, without regard to the feelings of others, happens often. You may be described as a hothead with a short fuse or a rebel. **In The Spread: Recklessness** indicates that you have strong emotions and often feel misunderstood by your peers. You love a challenge and are an independent person who embraces life. When **Recklessness** shows up in the spread is it an indication that you need to take it down a notch, pull back some and stop taking unnecessary risks. It advises you to be more considerate of other's feelings particularly when they only have your best interest at heart. When your energy is constantly running at high speed, you are just as out of balance as you are when your chakra energy is moving too slow. Taking the middle ground is called for now.

Resentment – You have bitter feelings of anger, animosity and deep ill-will towards others. You manipulate people and events in your life to achieve your desired results. Resentment is anger and hatred that you have held onto for so long that it has grown into a destructive force within you. **In The Spread:** Do you look at the world through bitter cynical eyes? Is everyone treating you unfairly or out to get you? Do you feel displeasure, hold grudges or go into rages for no reason? Are you just plain out and out vindictive to everyone and everything around you? Then you need to take a chill pill and find the cause of this behavior and get rid of it before it eats you alive. When your energy centers are this out of balance you can feel offenses that are imagined, not real. You are on the defensive constantly and if you really stop and look at yourself and your actions, you'll find that the people around you don't know how to behave with you. They act unsure around you and that's because they don't know what little thing will set you off. You can't attain any kind of personal or spiritual growth when you hold resentment in your heart. You're not always right, people aren't out to get you, life isn't treating you unfairly so just accept that in order to grow and learn you have to understand why you're keeping this negative emotion so close to you. Let it go to bring balance.

Sadness – Embracing feelings of loss and despair. Weakness, grieving and emotional pain are prevalent. You may be filled with sorrow over a loss, feel unworthy and unhappy. Instead of feeling the emotions and releasing them, you may find yourself holding them inside and becoming depressed. You may want everyone around you to feel miserable too so that you don't feel alone with your pain. **In The Spread:** This is a card of struggle. When sadness enters your emotions, you must feel the pain that goes along with the event that made you sad, move past it and back into normal daily living. When you embrace the sadness and hold onto it for too long, you can get in a rut of despair, which is more difficult to leave behind. Drawing **Sadness** in the spread is an indication that you're holding on too tightly to your emotions, trapping your energy in negativity. In order to bring the chakras back into balance make an effort to do something positive several times a day. Smile at someone on the street, buy some flowers and enjoy their beauty and scent. By taking positive actions to move away from sadness you are taking a big step in bringing balance to your chakra energy.

Temptation – It can come to you when you least expect it, enticing you to act out of character, to do things that you normally wouldn't do because of an expected reward or feeling of ecstasy. Not only may you be tempted but you may also tempt others in order to get them to bend to your will. **In The Spread:** Temptation can come in many forms. In this day and age of instant gratification, temptation is around every corner, just waiting for you. You may be tempted by another person, by the offer of a highly desired specific outcome or simply by that big slice of cheesecake on the dessert tray when you've been dieting for a month and haven't cheated. Regardless of the type of temptation presented, you must resist. When **Temptation** is drawn in the spread it is an indication that you are progressing on your spiritual path, you are attaining your goals but it's also a warning to walk the straight and narrow as you do so. Remain focused, don't be diverted. Temptations are distractions that can keep you from forward movement. This card is a reminder to stay true to your path, your goals and your beliefs. The high level of energy that surrounds temptations, especially when you act upon them, will quickly throw your chakras out of balance. To bring them back to center, avoid temptations. Should you falter and give in to temptation, forgive yourself and move on.

Turmoil – When life is in a state of turmoil and upheaval, you will feel restless and troubled. Your normal quiet life is disrupted. There is a sense of disorder and havoc all around you. You're unsure which way to turn or how to get back on your life path. **In The Spread:** Turmoil being drawn in the spread is indicative of scattered and out of sync chakra energy. It may be moving quickly and then slow down to almost zero movement, and just as suddenly be spinning out of control again. Drawing **Turmoil** means that you're about to go through a period of change and growth on both a spiritual and emotional level. This is the time to listen to what your guides are trying to tell you, accept help from the spiritual plane, recognize that you are but a tiny part of a grand Universe and your job is to learn your life lessons so that you may get closer to God. At times you may feel fear of the unknown because that is an effect of turmoil, but in letting go of this fear you take a big step in bringing balance back to your chakras and in turn, back to your life.

The Course of Action Cards

Affirm – Use affirmations to positively declare goals, be firm in your resolve, stay true to your beliefs. Give yourself positive thoughts throughout the day to help you stay on track. **In The Spread:** When **Affirm** comes up in a reading it is a sign that you need to give yourself more positive reinforcement to help bring balance to your chakras. You're doing a great job but you just need a little extra push, a reminder that you are on the right track, reinforcements so that you don't go off course. **Affirm** is an indication that you are close to reaching your desired goal so don't give up now. **Course of Action:** Stick positive notes on your mirror so you'll see them first thing in the morning. Pick a saying that fits your situation and make it your own. Program your cell phone to deliver positive messages throughout the day.

Attune – Now is the time to bring yourself back into harmony on all levels, including your chakra energy. **In The Spread:** Make an effort to get back to the foundation of your soul, peeling away the layers of self until you reach the purest part of you, your soul energy. When **Attune** appears in the spread, you have a choice to make. You can either make a concentrated effort to center yourself in many different areas of your life including all of your chakras, or you can choose to ignore that you're slowly falling apart. **Attune** is often an indication that you've been out of sync for a while, you've just felt off and not really known why. Now is a good time to find out the why of the matter and to correct all aspects that aren't in alignment with your soul's path. **Course of Action:** Take a walk, bond with nature, pay attention to the animals you encounter, take a hot bath, focus and connect with the water. Look at life through the eyes of a child, allow your inner child out to play, be good-natured and spontaneous.

Believe – In yourself. Listen to your heart and follow your desires. Consider you own truths, the parts of you that make you whole, your morals and values. Know that you are embarking on the beginning of a new path surrounded by positive energy. **In The Spread:** Drawing **Believe** in the spread signifies that you have reservations about the ideals that you hold close. This doesn't mean that you're surrounded by negativity but is a sign that you aren't giving credit where credit is due, particularly when it comes to yourself and core values. When you don't believe in yourself, it's difficult for others to believe in you. Disbelief in yourself can slow down your chakra energy; make you feel that you aren't equal to others because you distrust yourself. It is also a sign that you aren't steadfast in your way of thinking but are instead considering other options or belief systems. When you're unsure, you have to explore your world, determine your own truths. Curiosity is a way to expand your beliefs, to investigate and learn more about the world you live in, about viewpoints other than your own. If the new information you uncover fits your life path, then embrace that idea and make it your own. Draw your own conclusions and be sure of your convictions. What may be right for others may or may not be right for you. **Believe** in the spread is telling you it's time to focus on your own ideals, pay attention to what you consider as truth, regardless of what others tell you to believe. **Course of Action:** Follow your heart, do research, read about different philosophies and ways of thinking. Consider all options. Find a quiet place, somewhere that you feel calm and safe, and meditate. When you accomplish something in your life, know that you've done a good job and believe that you are worthy of the praise and accolades that go along with it. When you're able to do this, you will find balance within the chakra you're working on.

Chart – A map where you can plot your spiritual accomplishments, setbacks and growth. **In The Spread:** View your life as a spiritual journey; bring balance to the chakra by creating a chart for your life plan and spiritual path. When **Chart** appears in the spread, it is an indication that you may be off course. As you begin to analyze your spirituality, charting will help get you back on track. This gives you a visual to look at, to physically see where you've been, where you are now and where you're going. As you grow spiritually, you'll feel the equalization of your chakra energy. It may be expressed through a sense of peacefulness, a calm knowing or an overall happiness with everyday life, even when things aren't going as planned. **Course of Action:** Buy a notebook and some graphing paper. Outline your spiritual growth plan in the notebook and create a chart on the graph paper that you can color in to track your progress. Give yourself a rating system of one to ten on the left side and the days of the week across the bottom. Put the ideal, aspiration or goal you've set for yourself across the top and mark your progress daily. You may want to make multiple graphs if you have several items that you're working on.

Cleanse – To rid yourself of impurities and contaminations, to be morally pure, honest and fair. Cleansing is the elimination of undesirables around you. **In The Spread:** There are times in your life when you have to clean house. Not just the physical home that you live in, but your physical body and your spirit. Drawing **Cleanse** in the spread is letting you know that you've put off cleaning long enough, now is the time to address what has gathered upon you. If you don't clean your home, clutter can build up, dirt can accumulate in corners and dust can cover everything. The same thing happens to your chakra energy and your soul. Impurities gather, sitting there, putting weight on your energy. Physically, you may be contaminating your body with impurities through food, drink or a general lack of cleanliness. Get out the scrub brush and get busy. Look at your diet and improve it. Look at your spirituality and let go of anything that's holding you back. Are you ignoring your psychic abilities because someone said that you're not psychic? Take that comment and put it in the trash, just as you'd put the dirt you sweep off your floor in the garbage. That comment isn't doing you any good, but is acting as a negative influence, an impurity in your soul that is preventing you from expanding upon your psychic nature. **Cleanse** in the spread also means that you need to make sure you're being honest and fair with yourself and to those around you. If you haven't, then leave that behavior in the past. **Course of Action:** Simplify your life. Calm your inner self. Let go of the past. Soak in hot water to cleanse and renew the chakra and soul energy. Release regret.

Compassion – Sharing the sorrows of another, being available for someone when they are feeling down, lost or alone. **In The Spread:** Drawing **Compassion** is letting you know that you may have closed yourself off from others and from your own feelings. Instead of being available to share in another's emotions during times of trouble, you may find it easier to just avoid the situation and the person altogether. Offering compassion can bring joy because you are able to help someone in their time of need. If you haven't been compassionate in situations, forgive yourself for your lack of caring and decide from this moment forward to give of yourself to others. In chakra energy work, being compassionate keeps energy balanced while withholding compassion can cause slow rotation and make you feel off kilter. Compassion isn't just for giving to others though. Sometimes you need to be compassionate with yourself. This card is letting you know that you don't have to be so hard on yourself. Give yourself a break when things aren't going well. If you can't show compassion to your own inner being you'll have a hard time showing it to others. **Course of Action:** Visit those who are shut-in, donate time to community service. Take flowers to a nursing home or just go visit and sit with the people who live there. Engage in conversation, listen to their stories and let them feel valued because you took time to really see them. Volunteer at a day care or elementary school; visit the kid's wing of a hospital. Give of yourself to help others. When someone has a problem and wants to talk to you, show them compassion, listen to them and offer whatever advice you can. Sometimes you can truly help someone though a situation just by listening while they talk themselves though it.

Control – Keeping a tight hold on your emotions, trying to force others to do your bidding, not allowing life to just happen, but instead, trying to take command over all situations, keeping them in a mold of your own design. **In The Spread:** Drawing **Control** is a sign that you're holding on too tightly to every aspect of your life. Your chakra energy is tense and there is little flexibility of motion. It's moving quickly but isn't fluid, instead it is stiff and bound closely together. This is a card of letting go and of realization. Sometimes when you're so focused on having things your way, you may miss opportunities or people that you're supposed to meet because you have to be in charge. If you work as a manager or have a business to run, that's different. **Control** in the spread isn't about your job but is about your personality and spirituality. Clinging to things and bending them to your will is only going to cause the situation, or you, to snap eventually. By behaving in this manner you can push away friends and family because people don't like being told what to do all the time. You have to realize what you're doing before you can make the change. When you're so worried about controlling everything, you may miss the way you're making yourself and others feel. Back off a little and you'll find that the world isn't going to fall apart if you just let things happen instead of forcing your will upon it. **Course of Action:** Accept what you cannot change. Release control. Ask for help. Realize that your actions have consequences. Do something totally out of character, something fun and unexpected. Loosen up, let your hair down and walk with a spring in your step.

Convert Negativity - Release and block negative energy around you. Let go of people in your life who are negative or who do not acknowledge your true value but instead put you down. Don't dwell on negative emotions or behavior in the present or from the past, but try to see the silver lining in those experiences. Be strong, be a survivor and convert any bad thoughts or emotions into positive action. Remember that the only way negativity can attach to you or affect you in any way is if you allow it to do so. When someone is angry with you, kill 'em with kindness. It defuses negative energy. **In The Spread:** Drawing **Convert Negativity** is a sign that it is time to take the higher road even when those around you may not. This card is an indication that there is too much negativity in your life and now is the time to convert all negativity into positivity; this includes thoughts, actions, your environment or the people in your life. If you're unable to make a change from positive to negative then it's time to just walk away from the source of the negative energy. For example, if you are friends with someone who never has a positive thing to say, who always makes you feel small or bad about yourself, then it's time to make new friends and leave this one behind. The problem in this example is that, as humans, we always think that we can change others but that isn't true. Change can only come from within and only if the person wants to make that change. Take control of your energy centers, bring balance to your chakras and keep them balanced by making positive changes in your life. **Course of Action:** Take a walk outside, enjoy nature and sit by a pool of water. Water is a great conductor of energy, use it with positive intention. Connect with optimistic people in your life. Release negative energy and block negative energy around you.

Create – When you are creative you're making something out of nothing, bringing a new idea, product or situation into existence in the world. You can also create new emotions within yourself, emotions that you may have denied until now. **In The Spread:** This is the time to start something new. Positive situations and opportunities are coming to you if you'll just open yourself up to possibilities. Whether you're learning new skills or honing present ones, being creative allows you to connect to the Universal energy, bring balance to your chakra energy, allowing a deeper, stronger flow. The act of creation is a catalyst for positivity in your life. It is truly one of the highest levels of chakra energy. When you're lacking creativity you may feel as if you've forgotten something that you needed to do, you may be bored and irritable. Put your mind to work, use creative visualization to help you spiritually. You get out of life what you put in and by being creative you'll receive more than you expect. **Create** in the spread is positive energy flowing around you just waiting to be tapped into. **Course of Action:** Start a new hobby where you can make something with your hands. Envision what you need or desire and think positively about it in order to manifest it in your life. Create joy by smiling, even when you don't feel like it. Make music, learn a musical instrument, take a class and learn something new.

Deeds – Do a good deed today. Ask for help. Don't complain. Have pure motives. Doing good deeds gives a feeling of joy and well being. **In The Spread:** Things that seem minor to you may be a big deal to someone else. When **Deeds** is in the spread then it's time to do a good deed for yourself or someone else. If you always put everyone else first, then today do something nice for yourself. Give yourself a reward, even if it's just buying new music that you like. On the other hand, if you're always doing good deeds, take a day off. Overdoing it lessens the impact of your gift and people may come to expect it too much. Some people volunteer so often that they never have time for themselves. While it's fine to give a lot of yourself, **Deeds** is a reminder not to do so much that you're worn out and have little time to focus on you. **Course of Action:** Volunteer at the local animal shelter, hold open a door for a stranger, listen when someone you don't know talks to you instead of brushing them off and going on your way, give yourself a treat, go out of your way to do at least one nice thing for either yourself or someone else today.

Expand Your Horizons – Life is only an illusion, or is it? Look past what you know at this moment in time to ideas and concepts, places and things that you've never experienced. **In The Spread:** When **Expand Your Horizons** is drawn in the spread, this is a challenge to you on all levels: spiritual, physical, educational and emotional. You're self-confident, assured and are on the right spiritual path. Your chakra energy is flowing at a consistent rate. You will excel in any challenge placed before you. New information will be absorbed quickly and you'll find that this is the perfect time to start a new physical activity. This card is encouraging you to look past the mundane, broaden your perspective, develop yourself spiritually and build upon your strong foundation. By looking outward, away from the self, you can find hidden knowledge. This is the time to increase your life experiences and deepen the strength of the chakra you've chosen to work on. There is unlimited knowledge and exciting experiences just waiting for you to reach out and grab them. This is not the time to sit back and wait, it's a time of action, to take charge and truly experience the world around you and all that it has to offer. **Course of Action:** Read books or take classes online or at your local community college that allow you to grow spiritually, learn a new skill or further your education. On an emotional level find a challenge that will allow you to feel more than you're ever felt before, make time to do something that you've always wanted to do or visit a place that you've always felt drawn toward.

Forgiveness – When you can get over negative emotions, releasing built up anger or resentment towards another on all levels, only then can you truly forgive. **In The Spread:** In life it's easy to allow negative energy to wrap around you, making you hold grudges, anger and feelings of resentment against people in your life or about situations that you've encountered. Drawing **Forgiveness** is an indication that you have to face these emotions, acknowledge they are there, smoldering inside of you, and let them go. This card in the spread isn't just about forgiving others, it's about forgiving yourself. Have you done something that feels out of character for you, that's not your true nature? Take a look at your real feelings about what you did and why, write it down if you need to and then forgive yourself and move on. When there are things in your life that you need to forgive yourself for and haven't, they can keep your energy in a slow spiral, lacking in substance. This is a time of emotional healing, of spiritual growth and of finding inner peace through resolving issues. **Course of Action:** Ask for and give forgiveness, especially within yourself. Make an effort not to be too hard on others or yourself, let go of past wrongs, make peace with those around you and move forward on your life path. Seek out those with whom you've had problems, address issues, offer forgiveness even if you don't get it in return, and start over with a clean slate. Look inside and give yourself that same opportunity of a brand new page on which to write your life.

Fortitude – Courage and inner strength is the focus at this time. Difficulties may be coming your way, resilience is needed now. **In The Spread:** Drawing **Fortitude** is a sign that things aren't going as planned, the chakra you're working on is extremely out of balance, either spinning rapidly out of control or so slow that it's not accomplishing its task. During times of trouble you may get so involved with what's going wrong in your life that you forget to look at your energy to see how you can make things right. Sometimes things may seem like they're going wrong when the whole problem is imbalance in the chakra energy. Be brave, have strength of character and know that whatever it is you're going through has purpose. It may be a horrible experience while you're in it, but after it's past you will be able to look back and see the reason. Focus now on your own inner strength because you may need to offer someone else a shoulder in the near future. Drawing **Fortitude** means that you need to stay strong right now. Things will get better; just keep your chin up. **Course of Action:** Make a concentrated effort every day to sit quietly and focus on the chakra you're working on. Use creative visualization to imagine that the energy is rotating at a normal rate; not to fast and not to slow. Give your energy purpose and strength to help you through any problems that may arise in your life. During this quiet time and creative visualization exercise also give intention to the things that are causing you problems, imagine them converting from a problem to a blessing.

Greater Good – The ultimate goal on a spiritual level, that which serves your best interests, reaching towards spiritual growth. **In The Spread:** Exactly what is **Greater Good**? It is the ultimate rightness of your spirituality. It is the marvelous, compelling behavior that you strive for on your spiritual path. As you consider your greater good, it is the balance of chakra energy that helps you attain all that is yours in the Earth plane. When someone tells you to do what is best for your greater good it means being morally right, upstanding and ethical. You live your life with principles; you are honorable, respectable and trustworthy. You excel in life not by imposing upon others, taking short cuts or thinking that you're a marvelously talented person who is above everyone else but because you do what is right. You are an inspiration, people look up to you because you always strive to be upstanding, regardless of the personal consequences. When **Greater Good** is drawn in the spread it is an indication that you are on the right path. It also counsels to take inventory of your ideals and to place utmost importance upon continually striving to do what is best for your own greater good and the greater good of those around you. **Course of Action:** With all of the ugliness in the world today it is easy for people to forget about doing what is best for the greater good of self and others. Take time today to show random acts of kindness to people you don't know. Help someone less fortunate than yourself, even if that help is as simple as donating a couple of bucks to charity as you're leaving the grocery store, buying something that a kid is selling for a school project or picking up a dropped object for another person. It's not that big of a deal in your day-to-day existence but the small kindness you show today may help the grand scheme of your own or someone else's greater good tomorrow.

Hope – When you expect and desire something positive to happen in your life, then hope is prevalent around you. Never give up hope. Hold on to it and move forward in your life. **In The Spread:** Drawing **Hope** in the spread is an indication that you are ambitious, a dreamer, optimistic and that you look at life full of expectation. You make things happen by taking action. When a chakra is out of balance, hope can bring it back to center by bringing positivity into your life. Drawing **Hope** is a sign that you shouldn't let the negativity of others dash your hopes and dreams. If you've been going through difficulties and have given up hope, if you are thinking negatively about your situation, then drawing **Hope** in the spread is a sign to put these feelings behind you and embrace hope. Sometimes the fear of having your hopes dashed will prevent you from being hopeful at all. It's easier to not get your hopes up then to be disappointed if what you want doesn't happen. Being pessimistic is a sign that you're not allowing yourself to feel hope. Instead, aspire to excel and have confidence that you'll be successful. Have faith in yourself and believe that you can do whatever you set your mind to. When a situation is out of your control, allow hope into your life, even if disappointment comes instead. Drawing **Hope** means that your hopes and dreams will be realized, as long as you don't give up on them. **Course of Action:** Find humor in situations. Put yourself in situations where you can embrace the feelings associated with hope. Play the lottery and hope that you win. Enter a contest, set a goal for yourself and be hopeful that you'll achieve it and never give up that hope until you do.

Journal - Begin a daily dairy or journal to record your experiences. It will empower your self-discovery. **In The Spread:** When **Journal** appears in the spread it means that now is the time to start keeping records of your spiritual growth. In the past you may have just muddled along, noticing some things and trying other things but not keeping an active record of whether or not you were successful in your efforts. Drawing **Journal** means that you need to write it all down. You're at the place in your spiritual journey where you need to create documentation so you can refer back to it in the future. When your chakra is out of balance and the energy is sporadic at best, by keeping a daily account of your emotions, feelings, joys and disappointments, you bring focus to your energy and balance to the chakra. **Journal** means you're in a time of great spiritual growth and self discovery. Keeping a diary of your goals, plans, methods and experiences now will also help you in the future. As you begin the journaling process try to write something every day, even if it's just one line of how you felt about the day. Make notes about your dreams and any interpretations you may have looked up about them. Did you sense your guides around you today? Write it down and any messages that you received from them. Did you learn something new about energy? Write it down. Did you come across a stumbling block in your life? Did something go wrong at work? Can you convert that negative into a positive? Write it all down. After a few months of journal work, read back over what you've written and see how you've grown. You'll be surprised. **Course of Action:** Write down how you can change things in your life to remove negativity and blocks. Keep a dream journal, a spirituality diary, an emotion journal. You can use separate books for each or put them all in different sections of one book. The point is to write down feelings and emotions about your spiritual journey. You may even want to start a blog, but just remember that a blog is public, and other people may not be as positive as you or hold the same beliefs, so be prepared for negative comments. Jealousy has a way of snapping like a snake on the attack, people ridicule others when they don't understand a point of view just to make themselves look superior. Most people can see through these types of comments but they will still happen. Keep these things in mind if you start a blog about your spiritual journey and just turn off the comments section if you decide not to deal with them.

Listen and rejoice - To listen is to make an effort to hear something or someone, to rejoice is to show great joy and happiness, to combine the two is cause for celebration. **In The Spread:** There is so much sound in the world that it becomes something you don't really notice throughout the day unless it is a loud blaring noise that grabs your attention. To make yourself more aware of the sounds around you, sit in silence and then notice every little sound you hear. Doing this enhances your ability to notice the sounds around you. When you live life barraged with noise, it can desensitize you. Make a point to listen to a variety of sounds in nature, the sounds your house makes, how you breathe, the ticking of a clock and all sorts of different sounds. Choose music that is classical, new age, rock, grunge, hip-hop, country, music from a specific time period like the '80's or whatever type of music you enjoy. Then listen and relish your enjoyment of that music. When your chakras are out of balance, listening to the world around you and experiencing delight in those sounds can bring stability. When it comes to other people in your life, really listen to what they're saying to you. Be *in the moment* of the conversation instead of listening halfheartedly. By being fully engaged in the conversation, you can listen, rejoice in and truly connect to the emotions you feel with that person. **Course of Action:** Listen to music, sing with abandon and fervor, go outside and focus on the sounds around you. Live the fullest life possible and rejoice in that life. Create adventures in your life to bring happiness to you. Live in the moment by paying attention to and celebrating the life you've been given.

Meditate – When you meditate it is to connect with your spiritual purpose or to relax. Meditation is the method of connecting mind, body and spirit. **In The Spread:** Taking time to be with yourself, all alone, will allow you to learn your true inner soul and love who you are at your core spiritual essence. Drawing **Meditate** in the spread is an indication that now is the time to connect to the spiritual realms though quiet meditative work. It is time to ask for help from your guides and Masters, to reflect on your higher self. Accept your first impressions as truth and don't second guess yourself because when you do, you will follow the wrong path. Focus your mind on the lessons you have learned and the path you are to follow. Meditation brings balance to the chakra you're working on through deep reflection and focus. Applying these energies to your chakra stabilizes it and deepens the flow. This is a time of travel and exploration within your inner self. **Course of Action:** Choose a comfortable place to do your meditation. Lie down on your bed, sit quietly on a park bench, meditate in your office chair or sit on the floor in a formal meditative position. The position or place isn't the important thing here. Paying attention to the thoughts and impressions that you receive while you're in this quiet state of mind is your utmost concern because it will bring change.

Miracles – Do you notice the miracles in your life? A miracle can be small or large. It is an extraordinary event that stands out as a phenomenon, a marvelous sensation that is believed to be the work of God in your life. **In The Spread:** It's always been said that God works in mysterious ways. None is more mysterious than a miracle. They come out of the blue, when you least expect it, or they happen when you're been praying your heart out for a loved one who is in dire straights and needs help that only God can give. Miracles also come when you personally need help; all you have to do is ask for it. Noticing miracles in your life solidifies your chakra energy, gives it more purpose and keeps it in balance. Not all miracles have to be of an intensity that will drop you to your knees. Many small miracles abound in daily life. You may not notice them because you're too busy or because you're just not focused and paying attention to your life. Drawing **Miracles** in the spread is an indication that good things are coming your way, you will be energetically balanced and the future is bright. **Course of Action:** Look for miracles in your life today. Don't just look for big events like the appearance of a Saint in your window shade, but also look at the little daily miracles all around you; the birth of a child, a hard earned accomplishment of a friend, an unexplained healing, a butterfly landing on your nose, or a bird stopping to take a look at you. Miracles can be big or tiny but they're miracles just the same.

Nourish – Develop ideas, keep them alive and share them with others. Nourish your life and relationships. During a conflict, be the bigger person, let the issue go. **In The Spread:** When you draw **Nourish** in the spread, this is an indication that you're not taking care of yourself the way you should and your chakra is out of balance because of it. Are you running yourself ragged trying to be everything to everyone? Are you doing more than your share at work? Do you feel alone and frustrated? You can't take care of others if you're not taking care of yourself, you simply will not have the strength. Now is the time to put yourself first for a little while. Get your own energy recharged and balanced and then you can go back to helping others. You're only human; you can only do so much. Pushing yourself to do everything is depleting your energy supplies. Nourish means what it says, now is the time to provide yourself with the food you need for life and growth. This could be physical food if you've been skipping meals or it could be food for the soul that will allow you to become more in tune with your own spirituality. When it comes to your relationships, be encouraging, reassuring and supportive. You may not get back what you give but you will bring balance to your chakra energy and grow spiritually because of your actions. This is your lesson, your Course of Action, make it your own. **Course of Action:** Take a friend out to lunch, just because. Babysit for a family member so they can have a break. If you're overdoing it, relinquish responsibility to someone else for a while; give yourself some much needed time off. You need this time to recharge and regroup. If your sleeping or eating patterns are disrupted make a concentrated effort to get more or less sleep or to eat properly.

Patience – The ability to put strong emotions like anger and frustration aside while accepting delays, problems, troubling events or suffering. **In The Spread:** While being frustrated, irritated and ornery can make your chakras go out of balance quickly, patience can bring them back into balance just as quickly. Learn to be patient in difficult situations, with others and with yourself. Patience is tolerance. It is a skill that can be learned although many people are born with an abundance of patience. When you're able to accept delays, can stand in a line that is taking forever to move, when you can wait, and wait, and wait without losing your cool, then you've perfected patience. Drawing **Patience** in the spread is an indication that you need to do more work with maintaining an even temperament. **Course of Action:** Practice being patient in difficult situations. If everything is going well in your life and you don't have an opportunity to practice patience, then put yourself in a situation where you can. Volunteer at a daycare, have a conversation with someone that you normally avoid because they grate on your nerves. Try to look at situations positively instead of negatively. Know that this too shall pass and sometimes patience is the only thing that will get you through.

Persist – The ability to endure in spite of opposition and difficulties is the essence of this card. **In The Spread:** In all that you do, persist in what is important to you. Do not blame yourself when bad things happen, know that they are happening for a reason and continue your forward motion. Remember that complacency creates weakness. Persistence gives balance and staying power to the chakra energy. Drawing **Persist** in the spread tells you that when you feel like giving up, don't. When all feels lost, it isn't. When you think things have gotten as good as they can get, they haven't. Stay the path, have stamina and the desire to move forward. **Course of Action:** Don't give up; continue to carry on with the goals you have set for yourself even if it is difficult. If you encounter trouble look for new ways to achieve the same goal, take emotions out of the situation, look forward and keep at it. The way to success is in front of you, if you continue with determination you will be successful.

Present – There is no time like the present to address issues at hand. Live in the present, in the moment, let go of the past. **In The Spread:** When drawn in the spread, **Present** is an indication that you are missing the here and now of your life. You're moving too fast, doing too much and never slowing down. Your chakra energy is wound as tightly as you are, never going back into balance. Drawing **Present** means that you need to put the brakes on. Instead of rushing through your day, look at everything as an opportunity to grow and learn, by living in the present you are investing in grounding yourself, balancing your chakra energy and living in the moments of your life. Living in the present allows you to remember the smaller details of life. When you fly through the day, you'll miss a lot of things that you may have noticed if you'd just taken your time. Slow down, take deep breaths and remember this is all part of your spiritual growth. **Course of Action:** Make an effort to live in the moment. To look at what is happening in your life *right now*. Don't look back to yesterday or the day before but instead pay attention to what is happening on this day, in this hour, at this minute and second, in this very moment in which you exist. Live *in the moment* without thought to the who, what, why, when or where of the matter. Do it just because you can.

Take A Chance – Seize the day, grab possibilities and opportunities, be bold and daring. **In The Spread:** Whether you're taking a chance on someone else, on yourself or in some specific aspect of your life, you are trying to make something happen for yourself. Drawing **Take A Chance** in the spread is an indication that you need to be more free thinking, more spiritually motivated to reach out and grab what is offered to you by the Universe. This card isn't saying that you should put yourself into dangerous situations just to see what will happen but it is advising that now is the time to take action, not sit back and be a passive observer. Take full advantage of unexpected openings that arise, act quickly instead of hemming and hawing over what if's. By the time you finish comparing and contrasting the possible things that might or might not happen, the opportunity could have passed you by. Sure, some things may seem risky but taking a risk now and again can bring valuable lessons. **Course of Action:** When an opportunity is presented to you, grab it because it may not come your way again. Make the most out of situations that may seem mundane by looking deeper and seeing the positive potential within. Don't just watch life pass you by, seize opportunities, make positive changes happen for you by taking action.

Visualize – Use creative visualization, open your heart and mind to Universal truths. Put love in your heart to release anger, resentment and hate. **In The Spread:** When you draw **Visualize** in the spread it is an indication that now is the time to ask for divine guidance, to visualize what you want in life and see that end result clearly in your mind's eye in order to bring that desire to you. Whether it's a new job, spiritual growth, losing weight, or getting out of a financial rut; whatever the problem, you can visualize it, correct it and turn it from a negative to a positive and manifest it in your life. This makes your chakra energy positive and in balance if it's been off key. You can even use visualization to imagine your chakra energy coming back into balance and having a sense of equilibrium as it spins and rotates within the chakra. Your guides can help you during this process if you ask them for their assistance. But you have to ask, you can't just expect them to fulfill your every need without your interaction. They are with you to guide you, not live your life for you or to fulfill your every need. If that were the case then you wouldn't be here on the Earth plane trying to learn life lessons, you'd still be with them in the spiritual realm doing something else. Drawing **Visualize** is a reminder that you have control over the things that happen to you and that nothing happens without a reason behind it. By visualizing what you want out of life, you're taking a step forward on your spiritual pathway and are balancing chakra energy. **Course of Action:** Creative visualization is an excellent tool to use in many aspects of spiritual growth. You can use it to protect yourself with white light, to use the law of attraction to manifest things that you want in you life and to help yourself meet goals.

The Solution Cards

Abundance – There is plentifulness around you, you have more than you need. You have brought abundance into your life on many levels. **In The Spread:** Abundance is having a large amount of something, to the extent of overflowing, on a physical, emotional or spiritual level. When **Abundance** appears in the spread it is confirmation that you will succeed in attaining your desires and in having an abundance of whatever it is that you're seeking in your life. When it comes to your chakra energy, **Abundance** is letting you know that you will succeed in bringing balance to your energy levels. If you were seeking more enlightenment in order to open the **Third Eye Chakra**, you'll receive it. Regardless of what you were trying to gain for yourself, the **Abundance** card in the spread means that you'll attain your goals.

Acceptance – This is when you decide to give, receive or do something that you may or may not want to do. During acceptance you may admit that you're responsible for something that has happened or you may take blame. **In The Spread:** Drawing **Acceptance** in the spread shows that you have come to terms with the situations in your life. You have already made changes and will make additional ones when needed. You realize that you can't change others because each person is responsible for themselves and change must come from within. You have gone back and forth inside yourself to find the place where you can come to terms with your own spiritual growth and the balance of energy within your chakras. You acknowledge that you may not get everything you want but you will learn life lessons, you will achieve goals.

Actions – You take responsibility for yourself. You no longer criticize others; instead you help them with their problems. **In The Spread:** Denying that you are responsible for your own actions can keep chakra energy out of sync. Drawing **Actions** in the spread is a sign that you have done something to achieve a desired result. Your actions have worked to help you achieve your goals. You have resolved conflicts, adjusted your behavior and conduct in a manner that moves you forward toward spiritual growth. You have taken the initiative; have influenced yourself and others in a positive way. By recognizing that your actions have consequences and in behaving in a constructive way, you have brought balance to the chakra you were working on. Drawing **Actions** is confirmation that your choices and decisions were the right ones.

Awe & Wonder – Fear disappears, you live in awe and wonder, and you discover hidden knowledge about yourself and the world you live in. **In The Spread:** Drawing **Awe & Wonder** in the spread means that you may have surprised yourself as well as the people you interact with on a daily basis. You have gone above and beyond what was expected and have now gained great respect for yourself. Others look upon you as someone who meets challenges head on, who does more than just the bare minimum, someone who has the ability to invoke their admiration. They may be astonished with your progress and admire you for your accomplishments. You have made huge steps in understanding your own spirituality and because of this, you no longer fear the unknown. You have brought balance and strength to your chakra energy. You are filled with happiness and look upon your accomplishments with an inner pride.

Confidence – you speak clearly without hesitation or doubt, your confidence increases. **In The Spread:** Because of the steps you have taken on your spiritual path, you now feel strong and secure in your capabilities. You're filled with certainty that no matter what obstacles you face in the future, you will be able to walk your life path with assurance. You are more adept at keeping your own secrets and the secrets of others. You no longer feel the need to obtain approval from someone else to prove that you are worthy. You take pride in yourself but are not arrogant. Instead, you have become self-sufficient and know that you can trust yourself to do whatever is needed to accomplish your goals. Your newfound confidence in yourself and in your abilities has brought balance to your chakra energy and to your life overall. You now consider yourself a force to be reckoned with but you don't come across as conceited to others, it is an inner strength and confidence that makes you feel that your feet are on solid ground.

Connections – You are connected to all aspects of your life on every level. **In The Spread:** One of the most difficult things to do when you are working on your chakra energy and are trying to understand your spirituality is to create strong connections to your inner self, your spiritual self and the persona that you present to others in your daily life. Drawing **Connections** in the spread is an indication that you have achieved a high level of continuity between your spirituality and your existence on the Earth plane. You are becoming whole, your chakra energy is flowing in a positive way, keeping you balanced within all of your chakras. Now you are able to have strong relationships with people in your life without feeling that you're lacking in some way. You are sure of your psychic abilities, your place in the world and your path in life.

Contentment – You're content with life. You feel safe and secure in the world. You have a greater belief in yourself. **In The Spread:** As you travel your spiritual path, you no longer feel as though you need more and more in order to be happy. You are satisfied in your existence and your spirituality. That doesn't mean that you will not strive to learn and achieve more, you will. Life is an ever changing adventure and knowledge is power. While you will continue to gain more during your lifetime, the difference is that you no longer feel like a victim of what life dishes out. You know that you have choices and are happy with the choices made. Drawing **Contentment** in the spread is showing that you have reached a new level of satisfaction with your life and your spiritual self.

Culmination – The height of your achievements, the reward for experiencing changes in your spirituality and life overall. **In The Spread:** You have reached a high point in your search for spiritual growth. In your life, things are going well, you have a strong positive outlook and your overall happiness is evident to others. However, this culmination is not the end. It is a step along your life path. As you grow spiritually and take on different lessons at various points in your life, you have the ability to enjoy a culmination of your efforts over and over again. Consider drawing **Culmination** in the spread as a job well done, a lesson learned, a chakra balanced, a reward for all of your hard work. Culmination can also represent that you have embraced the psychic side of yourself or now understand one of the many psychic abilities that you possess. It is a positive card of growth and reward.

Empathy – You connect to the empathic part of your nature, you have more nurturing feelings and are more compassionate. **In The Spread:** When **Empathy** is drawn in the spread it shows that you identify more closely with your own feelings, you understand your motives and desires. You can easily identify with and connect to the emotions of others and because of this you can help them understand themselves. You see situations and people in a new light of understanding. If you are an empath, you have learned how to use your abilities as a tool to encourage and assist others. You now know how to control your empathic nature instead of letting it control you. You have found equilibrium within the chakra you were working on and in that discovery you have deepened the flow of its energy. You are stronger now because you took on the challenge of understanding and this knowledge overflows into all aspects of your life.

Energized – You have an abundance of energy, you're interested in trying new things. **In The Spread:** By bringing balance to the chakra you have been working with, you now have more energy and vigor. You are full of an intensity that others admire. You put plans in action, you are able to guide others along their life path and teach them to understand their spirituality. You're no longer afraid to step outside of your comfort zone and now seek new things to accomplish in your life. Your actions are powerful and have meaning; you are intense but not overly so. You're not demanding but are full of life. People around you may notice that you seem more alive and are living in the moment. Your happiness and vitality rubs off on others because you have become harmonious within your own chakra energy, spirituality, and sense of being. You affect others in a positive way.

Guided Protection – You are in sync with the spiritual world, your angels, guides and Masters are at your side, assisting in all that you do. **In The Spread:** When **Guided Protection** is drawn in the spread it is a sign that you've accepted the spiritual part of yourself, your psychic abilities and you no longer fear the unknown. You're readily able and eager to get to know your spirit guides, your angels and Master guides. You know that there is much to learn from them and you no longer fear their presence. Instead, just knowing that they are with you is comforting; they will protect you and keep you from harm. You listen to and acknowledge the signs that you are given. Through this understanding you have been able to bring balance to your chakra energy and are prepared to continue your spiritual growth with their guided protection.

Freedom – The ability to live life free of the restraints that others have placed upon you and that you have placed upon yourself. **In The Spread:** You no longer cling to the need for material things, for drama in your life. Fear no longer controls you, instead you control fear. You live your life with ease; your chakras are balanced and you make your own choices without feeling that you're out of sync with the world. You feel a new boldness for life; you speak freely without concern that others will think less of you for your beliefs. This doesn't mean that you've become rude and annoying, just the opposite, you speak with clarity and say things that others may deem prophetic because you are now connected to your soul energy and understand your life purpose. All is well and you are an inspiration to others.

Health – your health improves, you feel at peace with your body. **In The Spread:** Taking the initiative to find equilibrium within your chakras has freed you from the negative energy associated with your chakra energy being out of balance. You now experience a soundness of mind, body and spirit that you were lacking before you began your chakra work. You find that you are healthier overall, not just on a physical level but spiritually as well. Your life is flowing smoothly, you're not getting sick as often and you have the energy to begin new projects and see them through. Your new understanding gives you a strong sense of grounded awareness. You are at an optimal state of well being especially when it comes to your own spirituality.

Inspired Living – You feel inspired and inspire those around you. You live your life enthusiastically and this rubs off on others. **In The Spread:** Drawing **Inspired Living** is indicative of a greater belief in yourself, in your abilities and your soul purpose. You have found balance in your chakra energy, which has given you the ability to trust in yourself on many levels and to trust in your fellow man. You are more creative than ever before and new ideas come easily. You are a source of encouragement to others; you breathe life into new activities through your ability to stimulate the minds and souls of those around you. You give hope when all hope seems lost. You have obtained a connection to the spiritual realms and through this you are able to be a positive influence in the world.

Lightness of Being – Existing in a state of oneness with spirit; mind, body and soul. **In The Spread:** The experience of balancing your chakra energy has given you a light, buoyant feeling of inspiration and hope. You feel illuminated, as if you're glowing, and you are. People may comment that there is something different about you, that you seem happier and less stressed out. **Lightness of Being** in the spread is an indication that you have attained the essence of your existence in both the spiritual and physical realms. You feel as if you're light as a feather with nothing holding you down. You are free from worry, problems do not cause you to flip out or go ballistic. You understand that some things are simply out of your control and you accept that fact. You are cheerful and happy and don't take yourself too seriously. You realize that life is too short to worry about things you cannot change. You spread happiness and joy to others through your cheerful and peaceful demeanor.

Love – Love fills you and radiates from you. You love yourself which draws love from those around you. When you give love, it comes back to you tenfold. **In The Spread:** Love is the giving of yourself without condition, without thinking of your own needs but instead focusing on the needs of the people you love. When chakra energy is out of balance it is difficult to give of yourself or to even love yourself. You may feel that you are lacking something in your life but you may not understand what it is that's missing. Drawing **Love** in the spread is a sign that you have found balance in your energy and are now ready to love unconditionally. When you love yourself you have concern for your best interests, you understand that this is not a selfish act but one that is required for you to share your love with others. Love has many different levels and you easily express a deep affection for others. You have a tender, caring and a giving nature. You no longer worry that giving your love will result in a loss of control. You are happy within yourself and with the people in your life.

Positivity – You have a positive attitude and outlook on life. You release all negativity around you and don't make it your own. **In The Spread:** When you live in positivity you are moving forward on your spiritual path. Your chakra energy is upbeat and vibrant. In life you are optimistic and encouraging in all situations. You have released negative people and influences, use affirmations to keep you on track and are at peace with your psychic abilities and spirituality. You hunger for more spiritual growth and are certain that the growth you've already experienced will continue. Striving to be assured and confident is the norm now. There is little hesitation, doubt or indecision in your life. You know where you've been and where you want to go. You've learned from your mistakes and have forgiven yourself when necessary. The positivity you exude is absorbed by others and influences them in their own times of need.

Potential – Possibilities are all around you, bringing growth as you embrace new ideas, goals and abilities. **In The Spread:** When **Potential** is drawn in the spread it is an indication that you are well on your way to achieving your fullest potential. By looking at situations in a positive light you see possibilities that others may miss. You have grown personally and in your spirituality as you balanced your chakra energy. Being capable of developing new ideas into existence, being motivated and dedicated to your goals is common. Your enthusiasm for bringing ideas to life is contagious. You see things on a deeper level, to the soul of the matter, in people and projects. Because of this deep insight you are able to help others see the potential they have to offer the world, even when they can't see it themselves. Drawing **Potential** in the spread lets you know that you have achieved much during your chakra work; you're an inspiration to others.

Power – The ability to exercise control, influence people and perform tasks with ease. **In The Spread:** Drive and determination fill you. There is an underlying sense of strength in your persona because you have found your essence. You have brought power to yourself spiritually and you are now the master of your domain. During your chakra work you have learned how to exercise control over yourself and your energy. Now the ability to tap into this control at any time is within you. You are a leader, not a follower. People look up to you because they know you will not lead them astray. Just because you have tapped into a newfound power source within your soul doesn't mean that you're shoving it in people's faces, or wielding your new sense of power over them. You're not. The lesson of effectiveness and humility is yours. It is your inner strength that drives you, that enables you to take charge or back away as needed.

Relationships – you are positive, interesting and carry your fair share. You are no longer a control freak in relationships. **In The Spread:** During the course of your chakra energy work, you have learned valuable lessons about yourself. These lessons have enabled you to learn how to relate to other people on a soul level. You no longer feel the need to manipulate the people in your life but are more attuned to their needs. The realization that everyone has their own lessons to learn, that you cannot change people but instead must allow them to internalize situations, their own feelings and then make the change for themselves is clear to you now. You feel more nurturing and are balanced in your sexual energy. You no longer look at complex situations, especially situations with loved ones, as something that you must be in charge of. Releasing negative emotions in your relationships comes more easily to you. Now you understand that you can't make someone love you but can only give your love unconditionally. If that love comes back to you, so be it. If not, then you have given of yourself and that's okay.

Spiritual Awakening – You feel at one with God and the Universe. You connect to your own spirituality and inner self. **In The Spread:** When you experience a spiritual awakening, you feel it in every part of your being. You are now connected to your soul's path. You are open to new abilities, new thoughts and ideals that you once thought were impossible. Negativity is not a part of this new awareness. You feel alive and awake, and look at the world through fresh eyes. You no longer cling to material possessions but instead focus on ideals such as love and harmony. An interest in all things metaphysical, spiritual and mystical is of interest to you. Connection to the soul, God and the spiritual realm comes easily now. You have reached deep inside, explored your spiritual self and come away with a new perspective of knowledge that has been within you all along. You're more accepting of others and their beliefs. Exploration of spiritual matters continues. You are awake and secure in the knowledge of your own spiritual truths and this positivity affects all aspects of your life.

Stable Emotions – Your emotions flow freely in moderation and without restraint. They are balanced with all other aspects of your soul. **In The Spread:** Emotions are always in flux. They are complex feelings that are part of your consciousness. Some days you may feel in charge of your emotions and other days you feel like a total wreck. This is human nature and is normal in the grand scheme of existence on the Earth plane. Drawing **Stable Emotions** in the spread is an indication that you are in control of your emotions more often than not. Feeling sensible and resistant to sudden changes in your emotions is a sign of growth on a spiritual and personal level. You have analyzed why you tend to lose control and have developed the ability to understand the cause and effect of not being in command of your emotions. As you have worked with your chakra energy you have discovered that maintaining sensibility in emotional situations keeps the chakra stable. This realization enables you to stay focused and ready for anything that may cause you to behave irrationally, thereby keeping your energy centers in balance.

Transformation – The ability to make a change in your nature based upon gaining internal knowledge of the spiritual self. **In The Spread:** You have transformed yourself through chakra energy work, centering and focusing on your own enlightenment and spiritual growth. Because of this, you have transformed your ideals, morals, psychic abilities and the way you think of yourself as a spiritual entity. Transformation doesn't come easily. It requires hard work and dedication to understanding many aspects of your own humanity and existence. Drawing **Transformation** in the spread indicates you have succeeded in your quest. You have gone through a change in your way of thinking about yourself, the world and the people you encounter on a daily basis. This card is one of self-knowledge, confidence and personal development on all levels. Timing is an important part of transformation in that you could not truly transform your spiritual and personal self until you were ready and the time was right. By drawing **Transformation**, you are assured that the time was right and you have stepped into a new phase of your life.

Trust – To trust is to have faith, confidence and belief in yourself, in other people and in situations in which you find yourself. **In The Spread:** Learning to trust is a difficult task. It's easy to allow others to disappoint you because of their actions or for you to disappoint yourself when you don't live up to your own expectations. If you put yourself at the mercy of another, or feel an obligation to someone other than yourself, there is always the possibility that your trusting nature may be stepped upon and it will be outside of your control. When this happens it is frustrating, annoying and hurts. Drawing **Trust** in the spread is an indication that you now understand that while trust has to be deserved; you can give it willingly and know that should your trust be violated, it is not your fault. Sometimes lessons in life aren't always easy and this is especially true when it comes to trust. During your chakra work you have learned to bring balance though understanding, gaining knowledge and being reliant upon yourself. When dealing with others you have to give your trust willingly and openly. Know that trusting in yourself will not steer you wrong because you're placing your confidence within, you're relying on your own faith and accepting in your own ability to discern right from wrong. Drawing **Trust** also means that you are open, friendly and kind to those around you. You are good natured and know that whatever happens when you put your trust in someone or in a situation, it happens for a relevant reason, even if you don't find out that reason until later.

Vision – An innate perception of people and situations. Having a mystical experience where you see things and events to come, or that have already happened, with your third eye. Your creativity increases, new ideas come easily. **In The Spread:** When **Vision** appears in the spread it is an indication that you are able to see things differently and in a new light. You have a better understanding of the people around you. When in situations, you are able to see all sides and possibilities. You have *the gift of sight* and may see events unfold before they happen. You may or may not obtain a full understanding of these events at the time, but after they happen, the vision makes sense to you. You understand that not everything you see as a vision will happen exactly as you see it. Visions can be warnings, scenes of happy times or mental images of new people you will meet or places you will visit. It is important to understand the importance of having visions. It is an attunement of your psychic abilities with your spirituality, which you have developed through chakra energy work. You have brought yourself to a greater level of enlightenment than you've ever achieved before. You may also see things of a paranormal nature; you may receive prophecies from your guides or just *know* things that you haven't been able to know before. Drawing **Vision** in the spread is indicative of the growth of psychic abilities, understanding and using them for the greater good of yourself and of the people who seek your help.

That completes the Chakra Divination™ method of diagnosing and balancing your chakras. I have to thank my guides for giving this method of divination to me and allowing me to share it with you. I have found this process to be very helpful and it is my wish that you find it helpful as well. Remember to trust in your intuition and accept any help your guides are willing to give you when using the methods in this book. By using Chakra Divination™ you will be able to find the reasons your chakras have gotten out of balance, discover the Course of Action needed to bring them back into balance and a Solution that will keep them in balance. Believe in yourself and your abilities as you use Chakra Divination™ to become balanced and enlightened on your spiritual path.

I hope you enjoy Chakra Divination™ as much as I've enjoyed designing the cards and charts, the layout of the spreads, developing the meanings of the cards and sharing this method with you. I'd love to hear from you. Contact me anytime.

VISIT MELISSA ALVAREZ ONLINE AT
www.ChakraDivination.com
www.MelissaA.com
www.APsychicHaven.com
Email Melissa at contact@melissaa.com

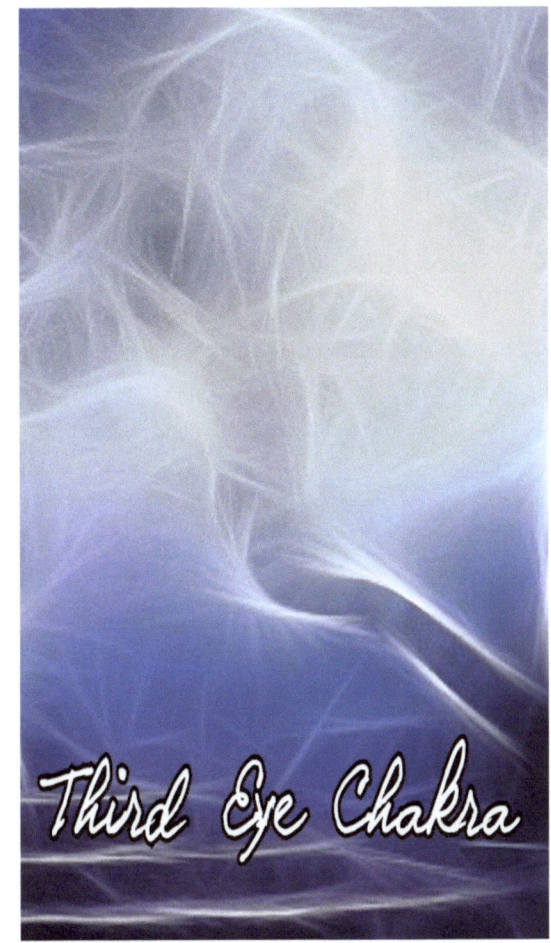

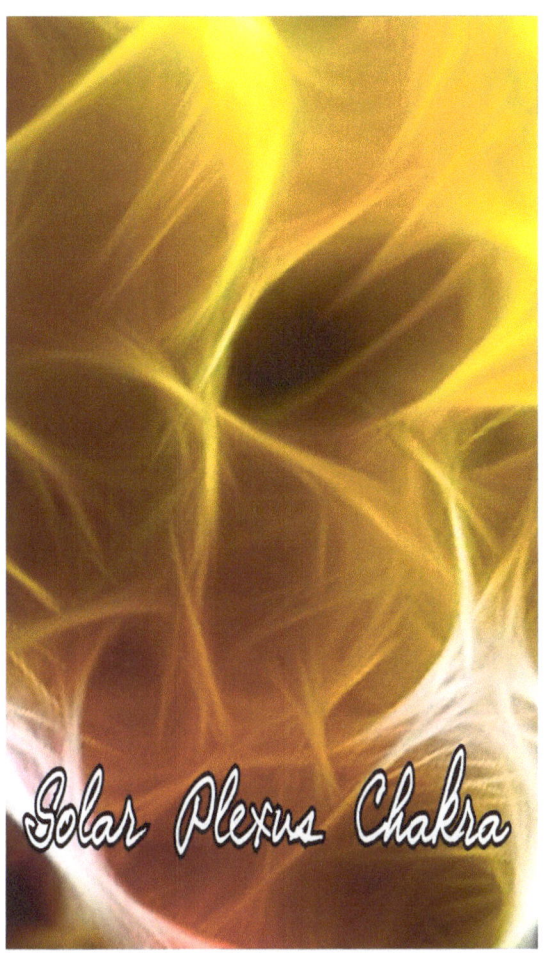

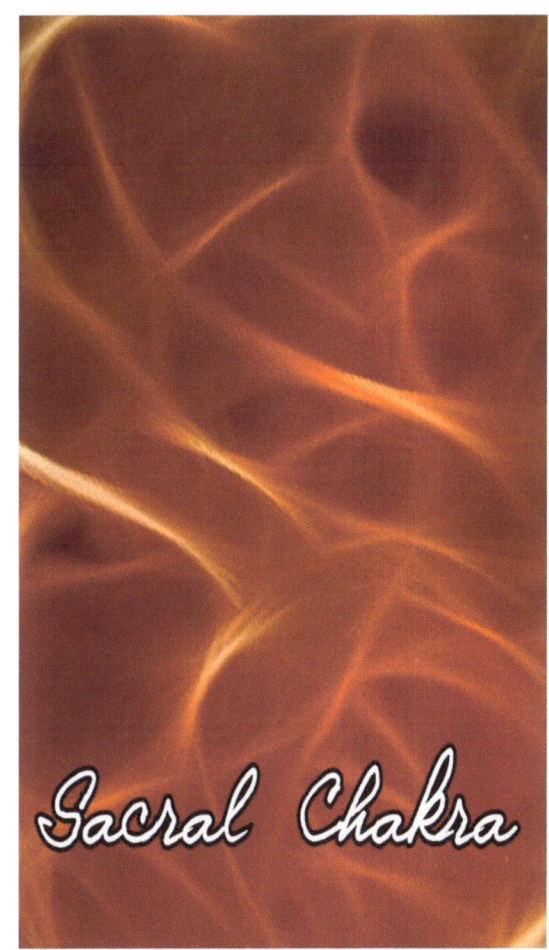

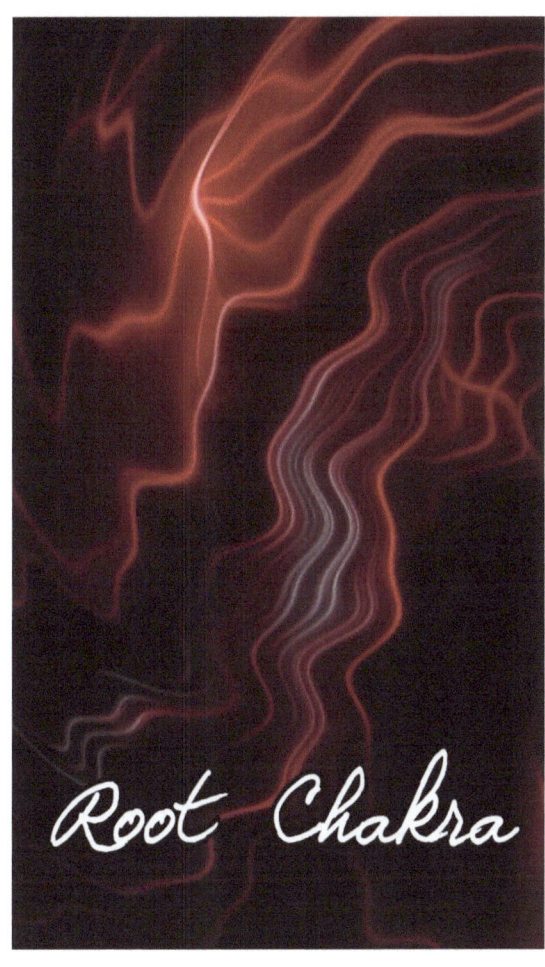

Anger

Anxiety

Avoidance

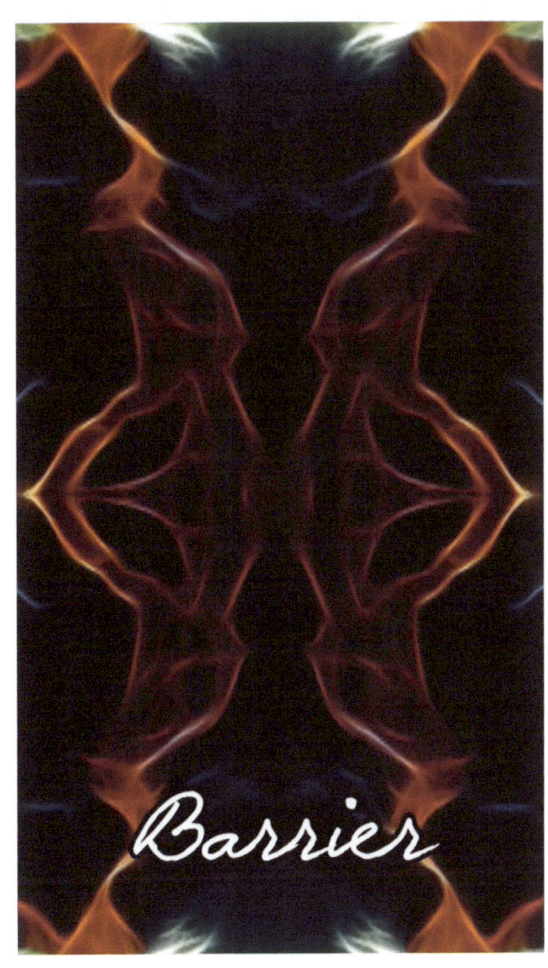

Barrier

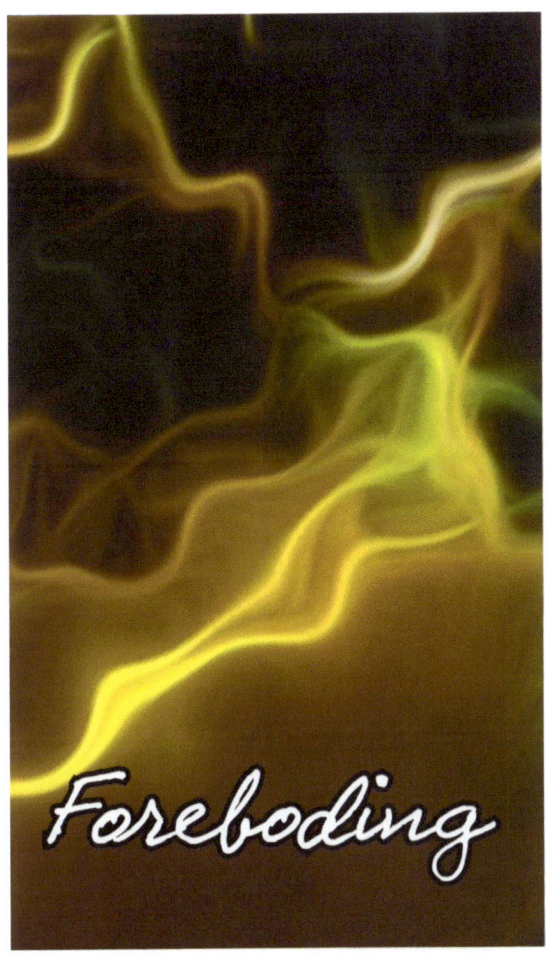
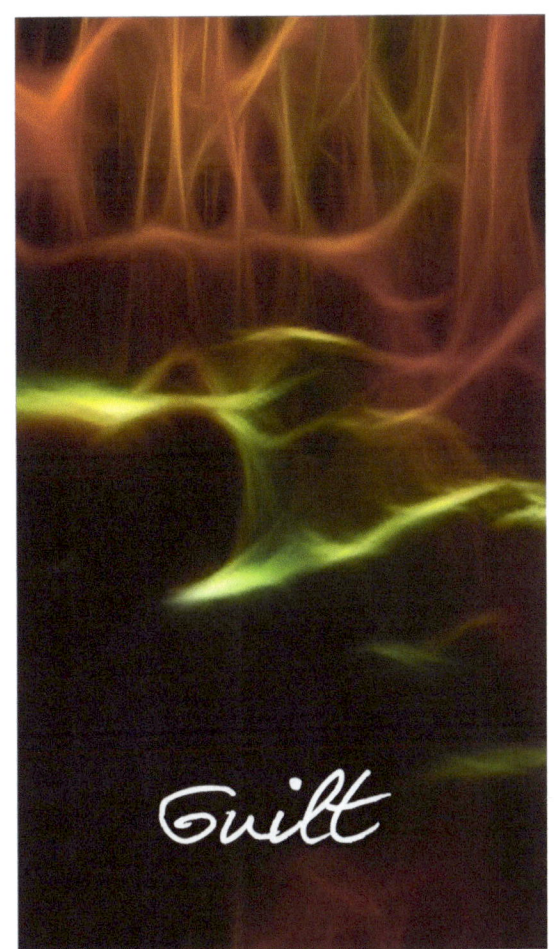

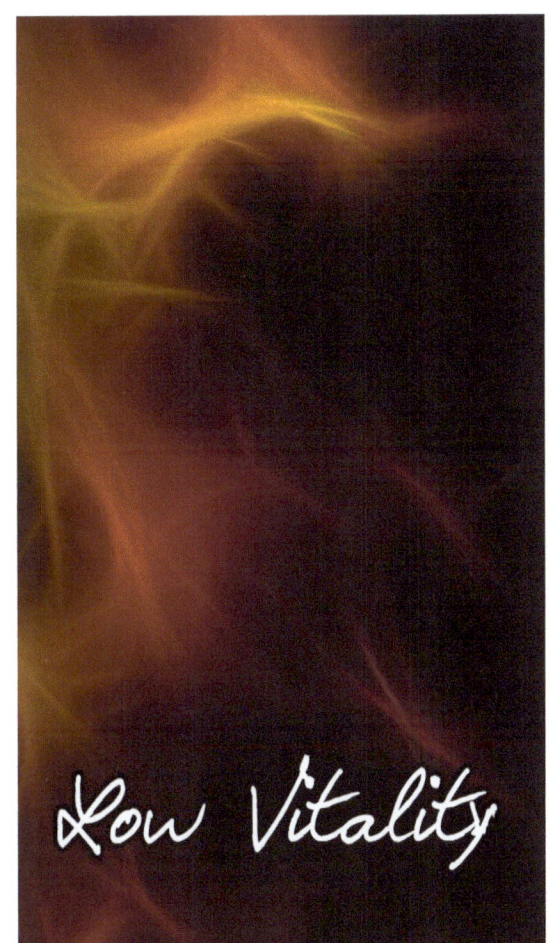
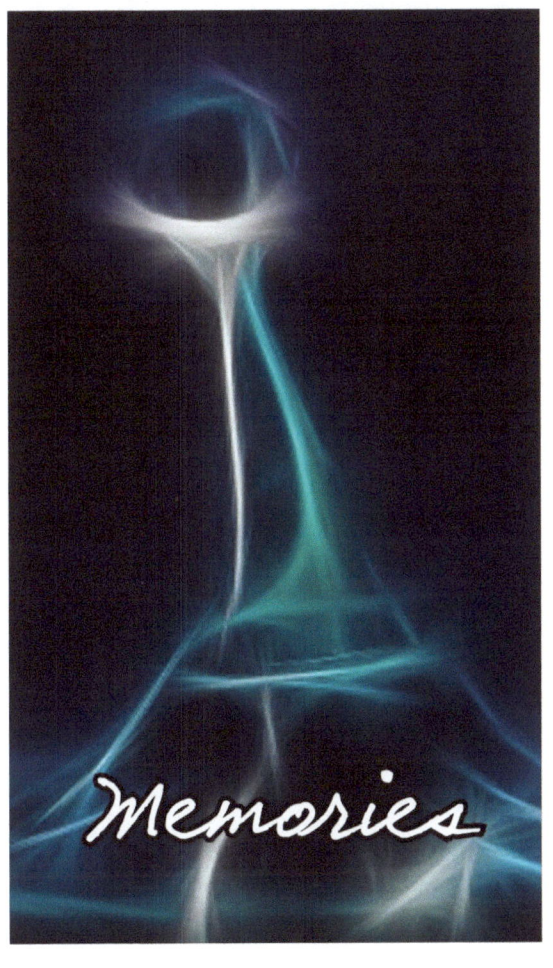
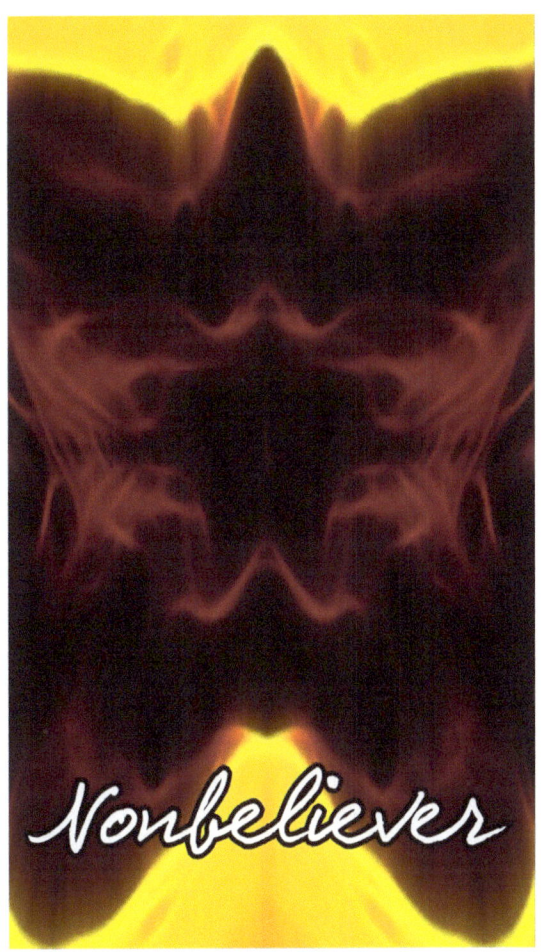

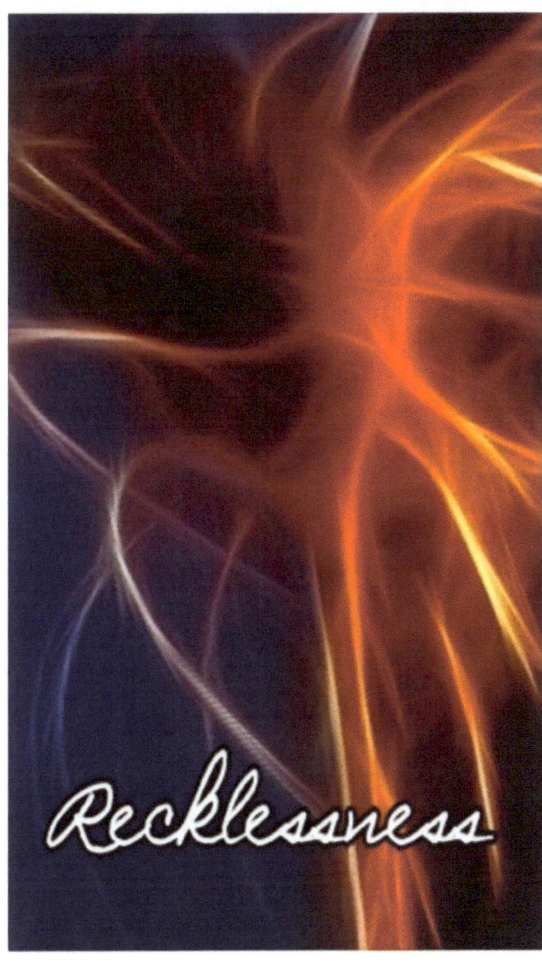 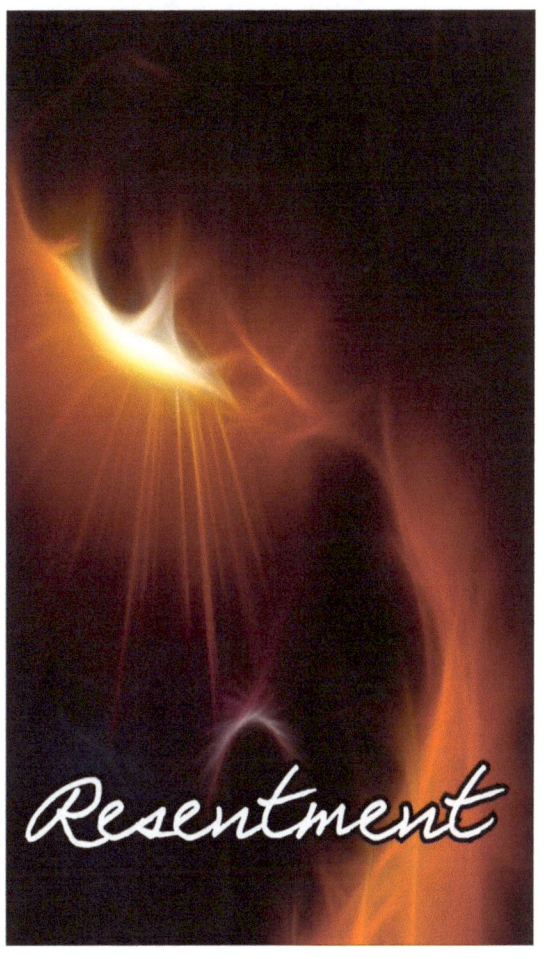

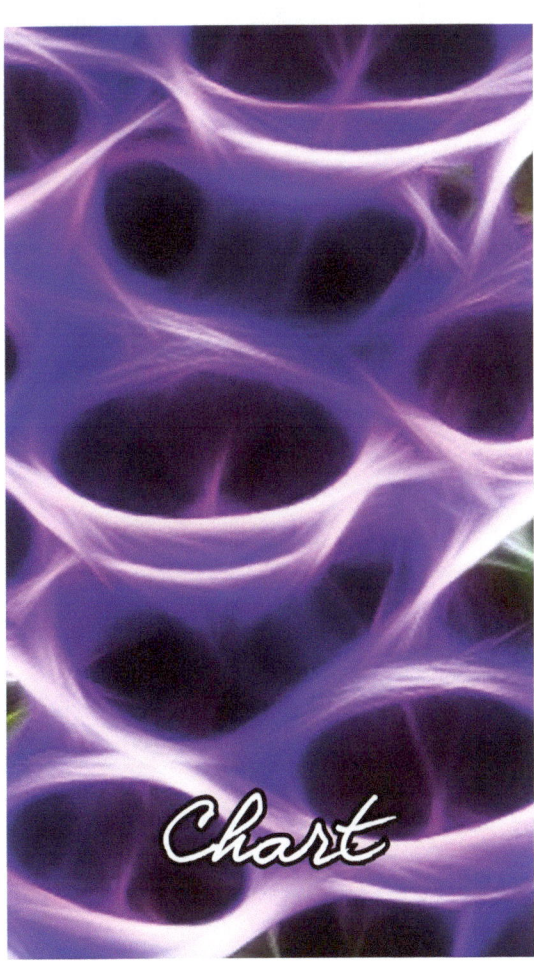

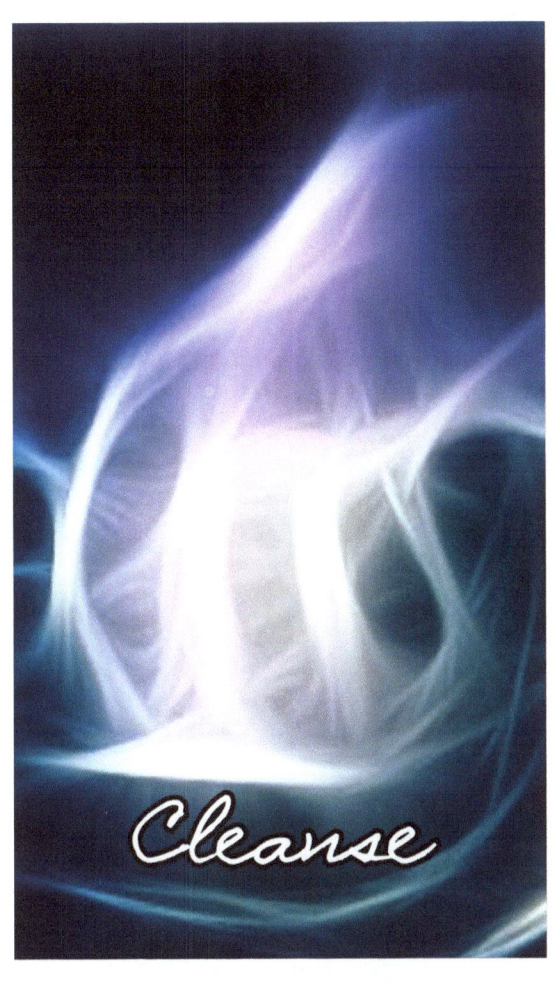
Cleanse

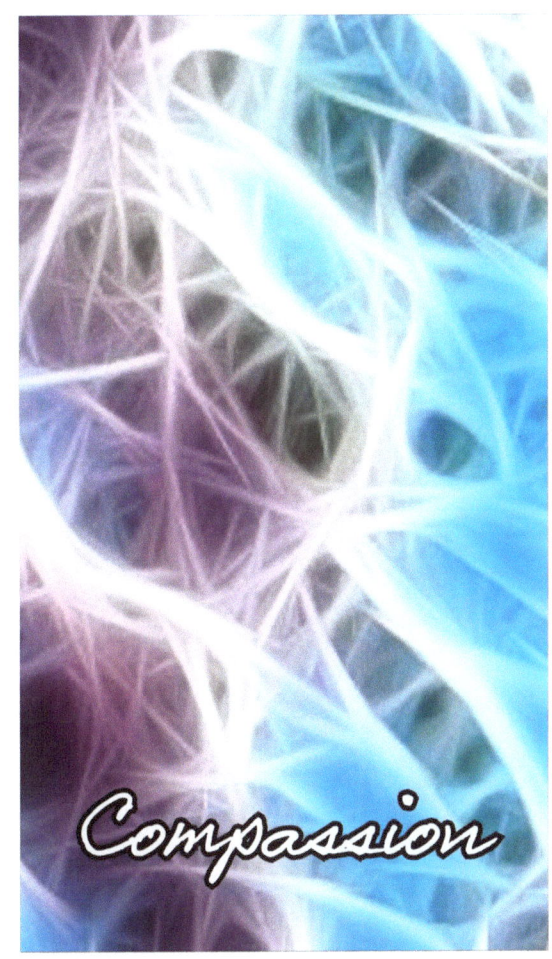
Compassion

Control

Convert Negativity

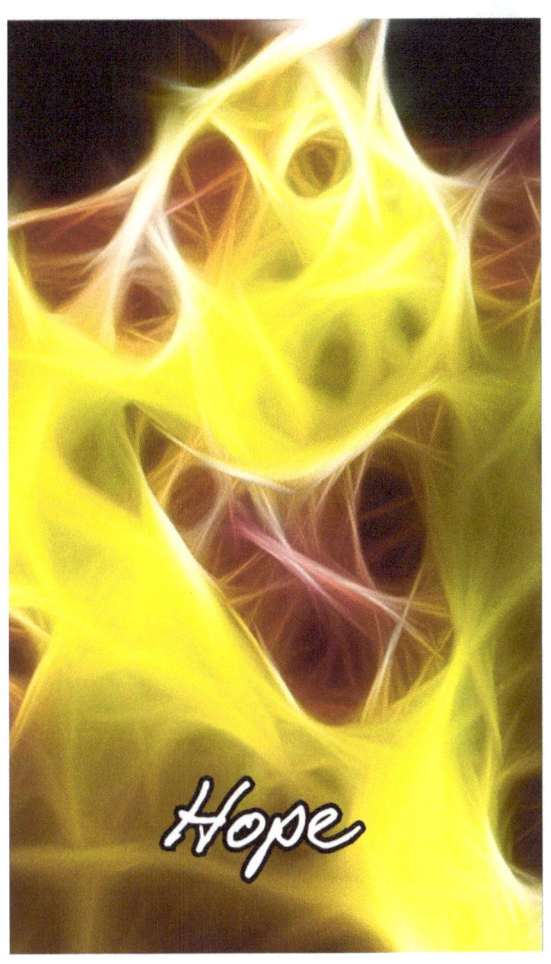
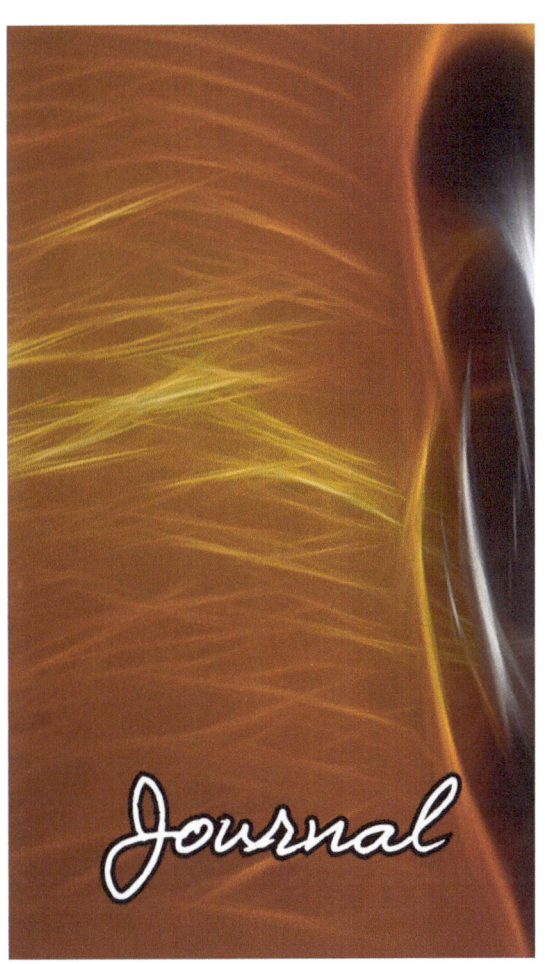

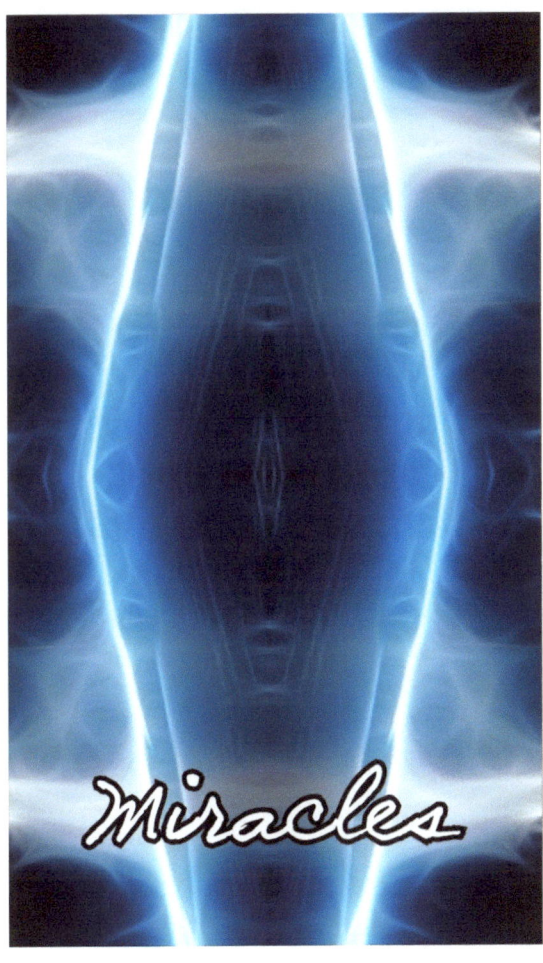
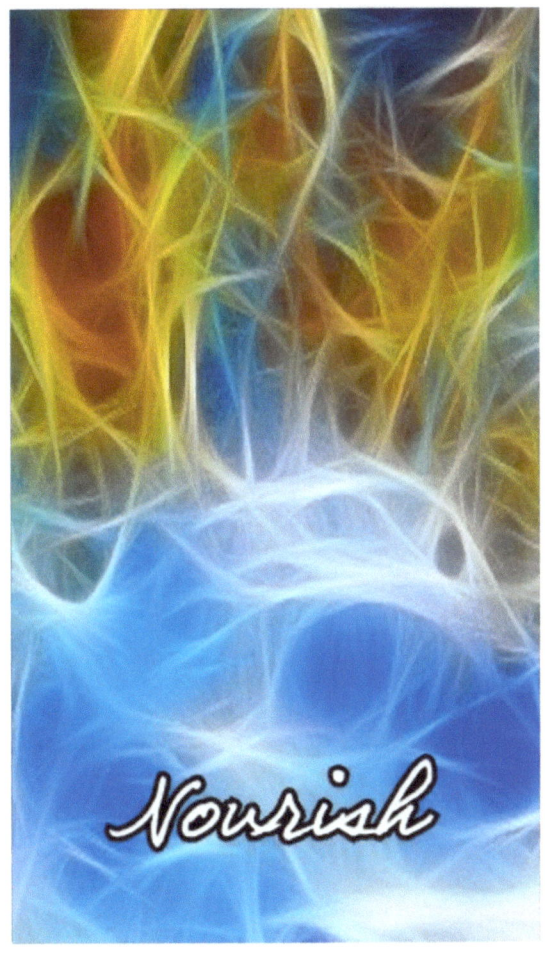

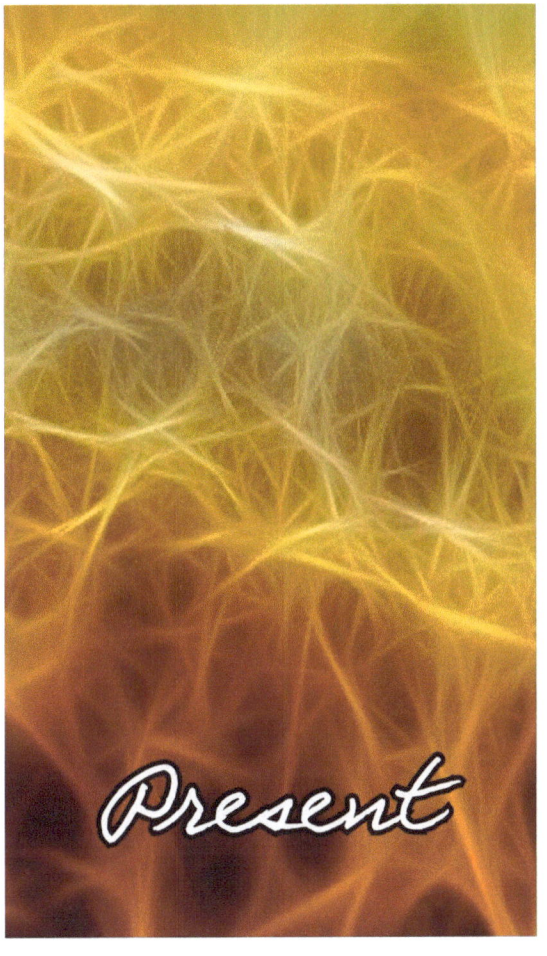
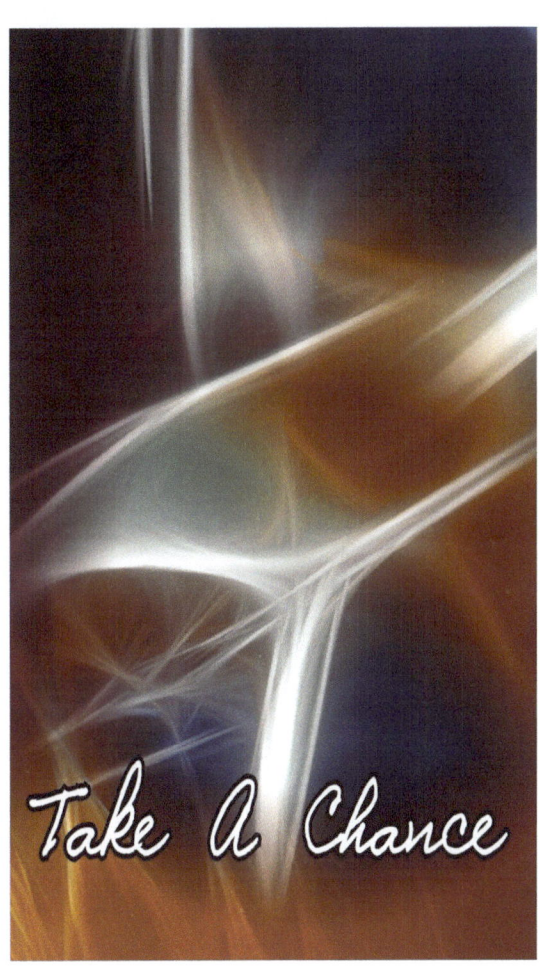

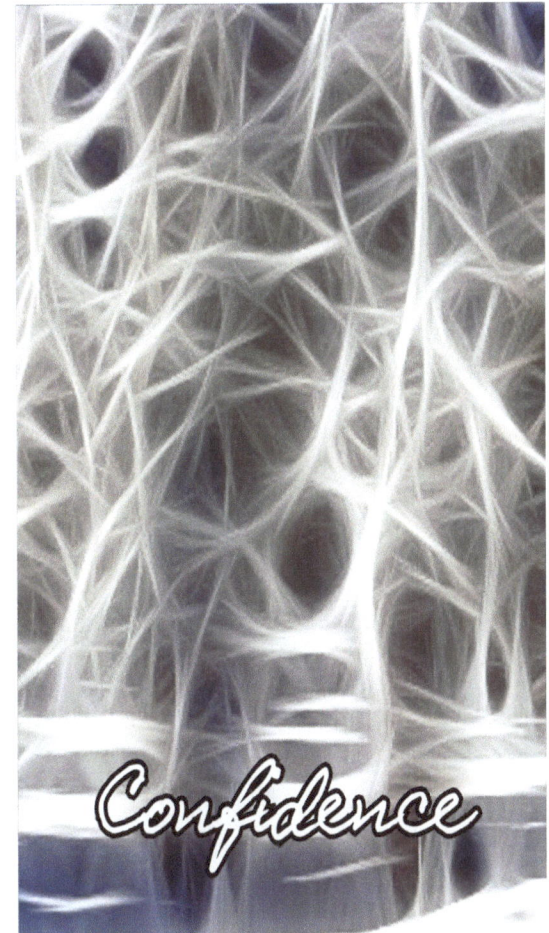

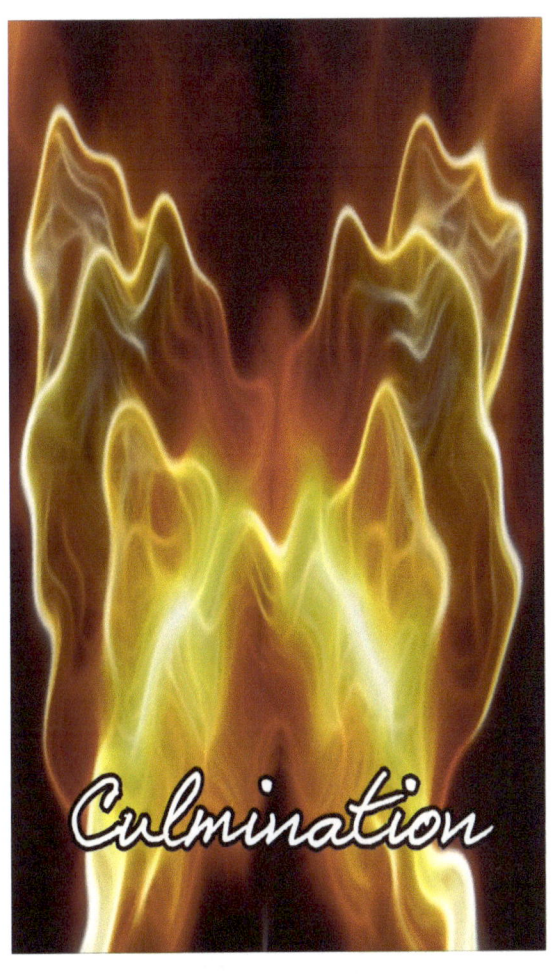
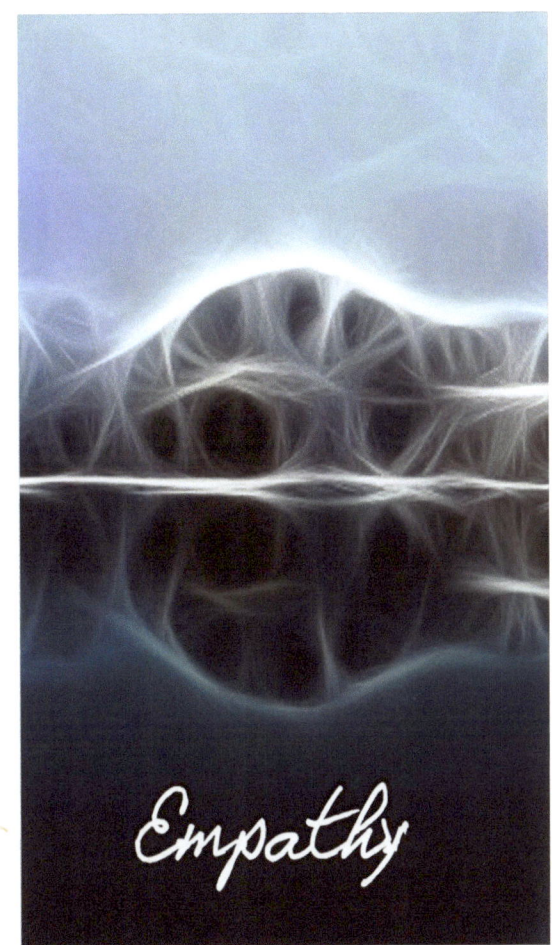

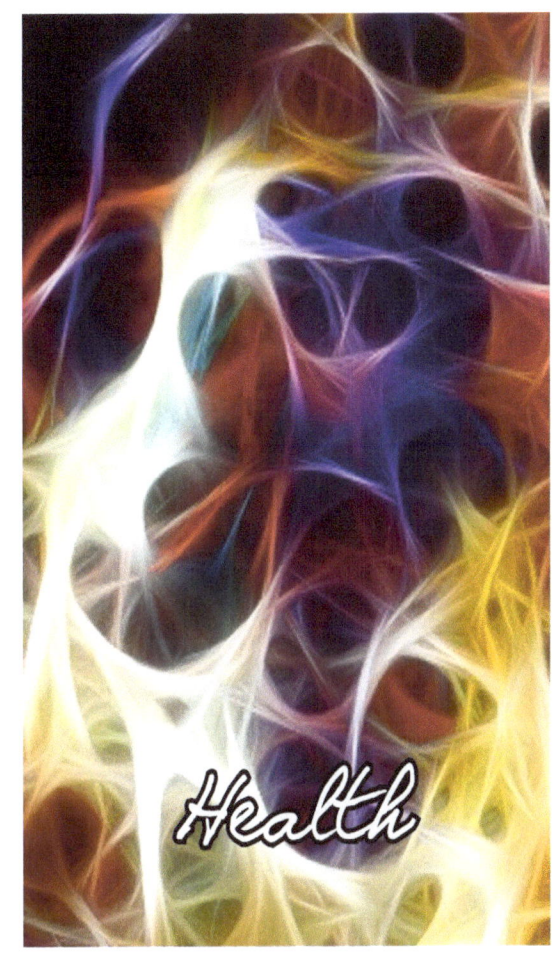
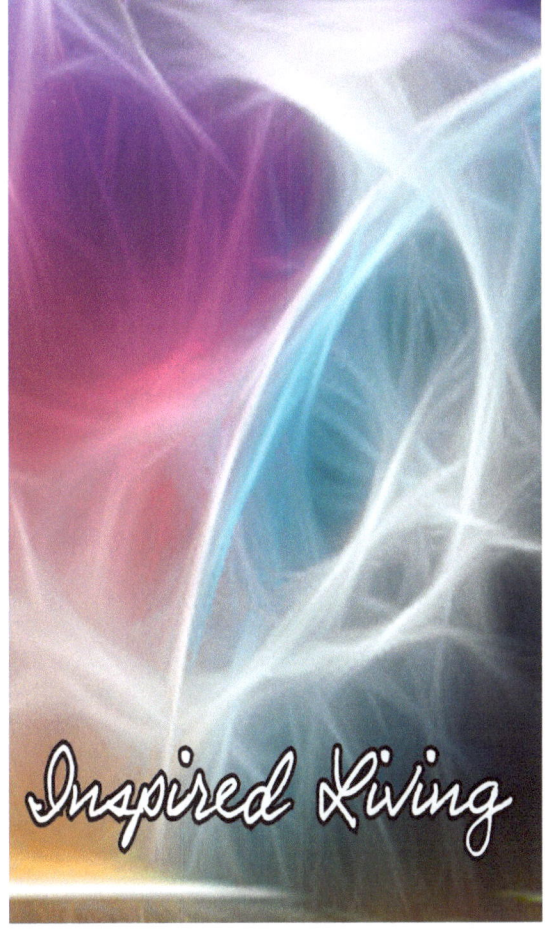
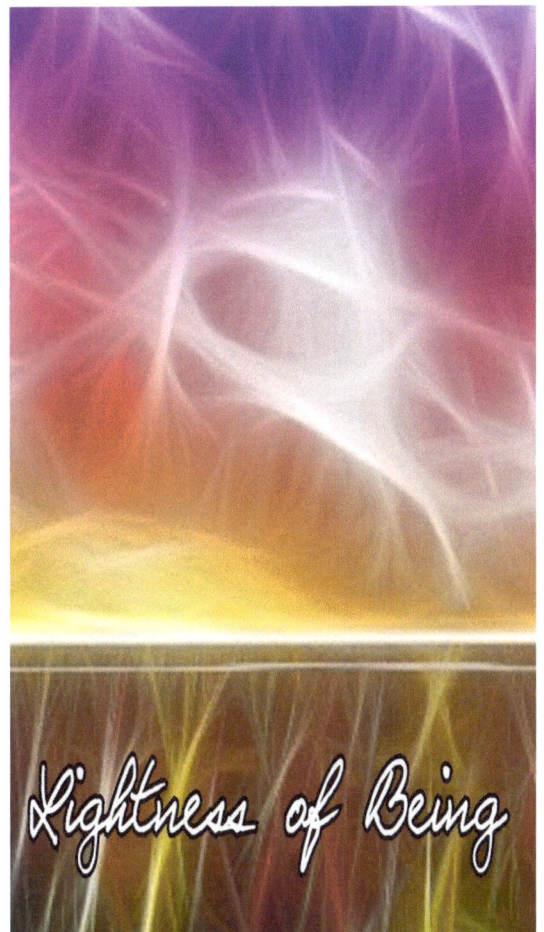

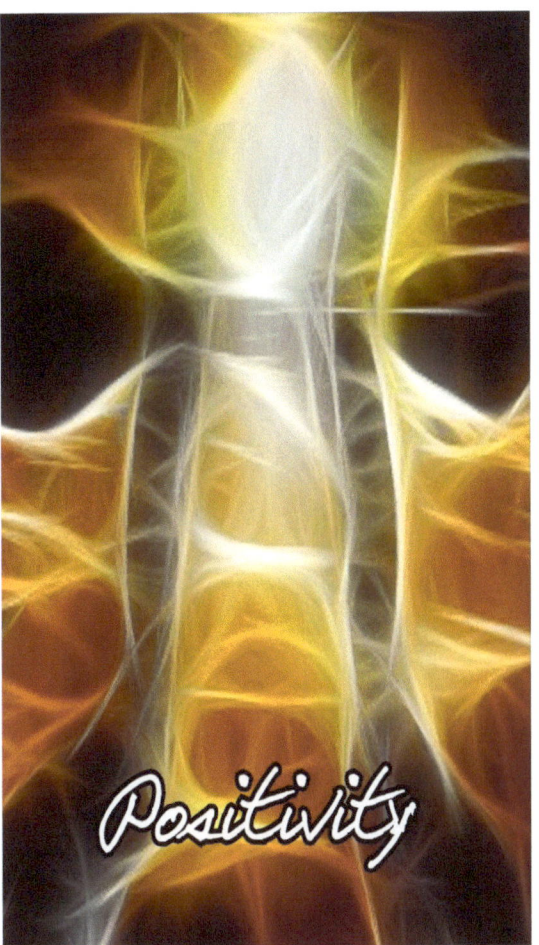

Chakra Chart

- Crown Chakra
- Third Eye Chakra
- Heart Chakra
- Root Chakra
- Throat Chakra
- Sacral Chakra
- Solar Plexus Chakra

Chakra Divination Cards & Charts

www.ChakraDivination.com

PROBLEM CHART

Confusion	Indifference	Illness	Avoidance	Foreboding
Hatred	Doubt	Anger	Chaos	Guilt
Temptation	Sadness	Absent Minded	Pride	Detachment
Memories	Lethargy	Low Vitality	Blockage	Recklessness
Nonbeliever	Fear	Obsessive	Anxiety	Resentment

Chakra Divination Cards & Charts

www.ChakraDivination.com

COURSE OF ACTION CHART

Believe	Compassion	Miracles	Expand Your Horizons	Forgiveness
Persist	Attune	Patience	Journal	Hope
Listen and Rejoice	Create	Affirm	Deeds	Take A Chance
Meditate	Control	Convert Negativity	Chart	Greater Good
Present	Fortitude	Nourish	Visualize	Cleanse

Chakra Divination Cards & Charts

www.ChakraDivination.com

SOLUTION CHART

Actions	Culmination	Trust	Empathy	Acceptance
Potential	Inspired Living	Health	Transformation	Positivity
Connections	Power	Awe & Wonder	Stable Emotions	Confidence
Vision	Lightness Of Being	Love	Relationships	Guided Protection
Contentment	Freedom	Energized	Spiritual Awakening	Abundance

Chakra Divination Cards & Charts

www.ChakraDivination.com

www.ingramcontent.com/pod-product-compliance
Lightning Source LLC
Chambersburg PA
CBHW042001150426
43194CB00002B/87